THE
DIVORCE
DECISION

92270

THE
DIVORCE
DECISION

THE LEGAL
AND HUMAN CONSEQUENCES
OF ENDING A MARRIAGE

Richard Neely

McGraw-Hill Book Company
New York   St. Louis   San Francisco   Bogotá   Guatemala
Hamburg   Lisbon   Madrid   Mexico   Montreal   Panama   Paris
San Juan   São Paulo   Tokyo   Toronto

1 2 3 4 5 6 7 8 9 F G R F G R 8 7 6 5 4

ISBN 0-07-046153-8

LIBRARY OF CONGRESS CATALOGING IN PUBLICATION DATA

Neely, Richard, 1941–
The divorce decision.
Includes index.
1. Divorce—Law and legislation—United States.
2. Divorce—United States.   I. Title.
KF535.N38   1984   346.7301′66   84-10033
ISBN 0-07-046153-8   347.306166

Book design by Nancy Dale Muldoon

To my good friend and administrative assistant, Pauline H. Jenkins, who was the mainstay of my support from the time I entered law practice as a young man, through my political campaigns, and for over ten years on the West Virginia Supreme Court of Appeals. I could not have had a better comrade.

THERE is the world dimensional for
Those untwisted by the love of
Things irreconcilable.

Hart Crane

Preface

Most of my experience in domestic relations has been with ordinary working Americans. The emotional dislocations of divorcing individuals are similar whatever their class. But while divorce among people with an upper middle class background—people who have comfortable salaries and career options—can be a financial burden, usually they will not find themselves unable to pay the rent or the food and utility bills. The problems that confront a university-trained elite are not the problems of coal miners, waitresses, auto workers, nurse's aides, police officers, or boilermakers.

In order to make the subject of divorce manageable, I have often had to generalize. Although I have tried to qualify my generalizations throughout the book, I have necessarily dwelled at greater length on economic problems in divorce—particularly the poverty of women and children.

This is definitely not a book about how to get a divorce. But it is a book about how to evaluate the divorce option in a systematic way, and in this regard I believe that most of its analysis is useful to everyone regardless of socioeconomic status. In addition I hope that the book will be valuable to counselors, doctors, parents, friends and anyone else who may be called upon to advise others. However, the reader should not rely on any specific information about the law in this book. State laws about divorce differ at least slightly in all fifty states, and the legal rules that I discuss are generalizations or composites. A person who has a specific legal problem should not look to this book for reliable legal advice; rather he or she should consult a local lawyer who knows the specific local law.

Finally, although this is mainly a book about how things are and not about how things ought to be, I have included some reasonable proposals for making things better. All the proposals that I address have broad-based political support and enjoy some likelihood of becoming law, particularly if more people come to understand the dimensions of the crisis that is emerging in domestic relations. More to the point, however, I have thought that brief discussions throughout the book of how things can be fixed may help highlight other discussions about how things have broken.

In the course of writing this book I have had the help and support of numerous people. The book is dedicated to my administrative assistant of many years, Pauline H. Jenkins, who did her usual careful job of typing, correcting spelling, and editing out unreadable prose through Chapter 3. Thereafter, my new administrative assistant, Betty Barnsgrove Price, took over these difficult and time-consuming tasks; without her enthusiastic help the book would never have been completed in reasonable time. I also want to thank my secretary, Tess Dineen, who worked carefully and well on a number of chapters.

I am also indebted to my two enthusiastic and talented law clerks, Sheldon Whitehouse and Kevin Brady. Much of the best prose in this book was written by them, as they tirelessly edited, rearranged, argued, and complained until they persuaded me to do things their way. In addition, Sheldon and Kevin checked facts and found the social science and statistical material that has been sparingly incorporated. In this latter endeavor they were greatly aided by our superb court librarian, Ann McNeil, who has a sure instinct where to find research data to support conclusions cavalierly set forth in the legal literature.

As this book was being written some of its material was published in the *Atlantic Monthly,* which exposed me to the incomparable editing and writing abilities of the magazine's staff. I am grateful to James Fallows, William Whitworth, and Jack Beatty, who as usual gave me a graduate course in expository writing. Furthermore, my friend Cecil Lang of the University of Virginia meticulously corrected the page proofs with his usual diligence to protect me from the many literary pitfalls to which lawyers are notoriously prone.

Finally, my editor, Cynthia Merman, made a major contribution to this book both by encouraging me to write it and by helping me to think about its content and method of presentation. Writing a book like this is particularly difficult because it is written for a national audience about a subject that arouses violent passions. In many respects Cynthia was more a collaborator than an editor: she tried to make sure that the book would be responsive to the needs of readers whose problems are remote from my own experience, and she was constantly concerned that the way things were said not distract readers from what was said. To the extent that errors or judgmental remarks remain, however, responsibility for them is of course my own.

Fairmont, West Virginia
June 13, 1984

Contents

Preface   ix

1 The Fading Consensus   I

2 Abstracting Life into Law   29

3 Child Custody   58

4 Paying for Divorce   87

5 When to Hire a Lawyer, When to Go to Court,
and When to Settle   119

6 Marriage Contracts, Living Together,
and Palimony   144

7 The Bottom Line   174

Index   199

1

The Fading Consensus

APPROXIMATELY half of all the civil cases heard in the major state courts involve domestic matters, and if current trends continue, roughly three out of every five marriages begun in the 1980s will end in divorce. It is not surprising, therefore, that a state civil court's most important function, at least with respect to the number of lives touched, is the resolution of family matters.

Satisfaction with our domestic courts, however, is at an all-time low. A person who goes to domestic court with a contested case seldom emerges with the reassuring impression that justice has been done. The most satisfied users submit their own agreements to the court for a "rubber-stamp" approval. Such consensual arrangements are fairly common, but the cases that trouble us are those which require a judge to award custody, set alimony and child support, and divide property. Where emotions run high and these matters are hotly contested, the arrangements provided by a court are seldom satisfactory, even to the so-called winning party.

The performance of domestic courts can be improved. Much of their poor performance comes from inadequate supporting resources, such as prosecutors to enforce child support awards, and from complicated procedures that both delay decisions and confuse the issues to be decided. Also, domestic courts fail for reasons that have nothing to do with the courts themselves.

Often the domestic courts are asked to do the impossible—to arrange a satisfactory child custody plan when one parent lives in Hollywood and the other lives in New York City, for example. Where the issue is money, as it often is, how does a court squeeze adequate child support from a man who makes only $1,200 a month before taxes? And, if that man leaves home and flees to another state, how does a court find him to enforce its order? Finally, no domestic court can repeal the law of economy of scale that governs joint households. From a purely financial perspective, when a married couple break up and move to separate residences, it is impossible for them to duplicate the quality of life they enjoyed while living together.

Marriage has certain economic and cultural advantages that cannot be replaced by even the most perfect court order. On the simplest level, utilities are cheaper when people live together. One telephone adequately serves most households, while heating hot water, cooking, and lighting cost less per person when shared. Although most households have two cars, insurance is cheaper per car when two or more are insured together, and less gasoline is used because travel is consolidated. It is usually cheaper to buy or rent one house than two apartments, and a large house or apartment is not twice as expensive as two small ones. The cost of fire and liability insurance for a couple is only about 65 percent of what it is for two people living in separate households. Family vacations are cheaper per person than individual ones; food is cheaper per person when prepared for two or more; and one stereo, television set, washer, drier, iron, and the like usually suffices for a family of four.

These economies of scale relate to savings on direct cash outlays. There are other economies of scale that relate to quality of life and leisure. For example, most households have a well-defined division of labor. Although there is no reason that a woman cannot fix a car or a man make an outstanding beef stew, the usual division of labor is the other way around. It takes training both to fix a car and to make a stew, and at the benign level that exists in most marriages arbitrary division of labor based on sex assures specialized training in complementary skills. In the ordinary American scheme of things, when couples divorce, men must cook, do laundry, care for children, shop for groceries, and a host of other things that used to be done for them. Women, on the other hand, must maintain cars, repair plumbing, mow yards, and do other traditionally male jobs. Most divorced people living alone manage to make do for themselves, but they must work much harder than married couples do at the ordinary chores of living, and single heads of households work the hardest of all.

Finally, there are advantages to married life that have nothing to do with either money or division of labor. Family life provides a support network that is difficult to duplicate. When a person has parents, siblings, and collateral relatives, he or she need not rely entirely on the nuclear family of spouse and children for emotional support. When a person's only close relatives are his or her spouse and children, however, the loss of their companionship and emotional support is irreplaceable, at least in the short run.

Domestic courts are considered unsatisfactory because they are expected to do what they cannot do: create a viable economic substitute for marriage. Contrary to popular conception, a domestic court's powers are extremely limited. All a domestic court can do is decide whether a divorce is proper, how much money should be paid on a continuing basis by one partner to the other, how property should be divided, and who should have custody of the children. What a domestic court cannot do is get both parties higher-paying jobs to defray the new expenses of separate living, train them how to live without the complementary skills of a partner, or create a new emotional support system. Nor can a court prevent one parent from turning the children against the other parent or guarantee the quality of a new family that children may enter if a parent remarries.

Most divorcing couples understand the limits of a domestic court's powers. Yet there is still a pervasive dissatisfaction with what these courts do. It is almost universally thought that in awarding child custody, setting child support, alimony, and dividing property domestic courts behave in a high-handed, arbitrary, and unjust way. Part of this complaint is a response to the relative poverty, inconvenience, and emotional voids that divorce creates. Another and more justified part comes from our lack of consensus about what constitutes fairness and justice in domestic matters. A court cannot do justice unless it has some clear guidance about what justice is. At the moment, that guidance is lacking.

Domestic relations litigation has two distinct aspects, the economic and the emotional. The economic issues involve making provision for children and a wife who may have no work experience. The emotional issues involve determining relative degrees of fault in the breakup of the marriage and molding decisions about alimony and child custody to take account of fault. The questions that domestic courts are asked to decide are neither clearly economic nor clearly emotional. Much of the apparent caprice of domestic courts is a consequence of the conflict inherent in trying to achieve fair economic results and fair emotional results simultaneously.

Our lack of consensus about justice in domestic matters is relatively recent. Thirty years ago marriage with one partner for life was considered the norm; any deviation required extraordinary circumstances to justify it. Such a sanctity, however, is no longer attributed to marriage by a majority of Americans. Some religions, particularly Roman Catholicism, still perceive marriage as a "sacrament," but lack of majority support for that position prevents its being reflected in the formal legal structure. Yet thirty years ago, the divorce laws of almost all the states (Nevada being the notorious exception) mirrored a social consensus that marriage for life was an institution ordained by God.

Furthermore, the entire legal and social structure reinforced marriage as a sacred institution. Premarital and extramarital sex were frowned upon; colleges prohibited members of the opposite sex from visiting one anothers' dormitory rooms; many hotels and boardinghouses discouraged "immoral" behavior on their premises; high schools expelled married students to maintain the sexual innocence of the unmarried; and almost everywhere sexual relations between unmarried persons were prohibited by law even if the law was seldom enforced.

At another level, employers looked carefully at the family lives of their employees. Unmarried employees found fewer opportunities for advancement, and a person who divorced for reasons related to his or her misconduct, such as the desire to marry a lover, often found himself or herself ostracized. Today it is illegal even to *inquire* about a potential employee's marital status. Of course, this history, like all history, is largely generalization. The social pressures encouraging straitlaced behavior were more intense on middle-class managers than on day laborers or factory workers. Itinerant people and people living in big cities, where comparative anonymity is possible, had fewer pressures than did those living in small, tightly knit communities.

There was, however, a strong enough consensus about the sanctity of marriage, the proper roles of men and women within a marriage, and the reasons justifying divorce, that we had manageable standards for the courts to apply in order to achieve what both winners and losers largely agreed was justice. In the first place, the available grounds for divorce were limited and concrete. In general they consisted of adultery, alcoholism, conviction of a felony, desertion, incurable insanity, and physical and mental cruelty. Divorce laws were intentionally designed to make divorce difficult and unattractive in order to enhance the stability of marriage. In some states neither insanity nor mental cruelty made the list.

The narrowness of the legal grounds for divorce, and their concrete rather than speculative nature, made it difficult, or at least expensive, for men to trade in their wives for newer models. If a wife was not guilty of one of the enumerated grounds that constituted fault, her husband could not divorce her. If he wanted a divorce, she, however, could very likely divorce him because he was probably guilty of adultery, abandonment, or cruelty. Thus, a philandering husband could get a divorce only with his wife's acquiescence, and that meant agreeing to her terms. While a man could move to Nevada and get a quickie divorce, that was all he could get. The wife kept the property and the children that were in the home state, and often the home state would not recognize a Nevada divorce.

The major flaw in the old system was that the disincentives to divorce were effective in direct proportion to the couple's income and position in the community. Husbands or wives without property or economic opportunities that tied them to their native regions could move permanently to a state with liberal divorce laws and, by so doing, escape the system. And where both husband and wife wanted a divorce and there was no contest over children or property, they could usually find a friendly court that would wink at many of the technical rules.

Women were discouraged from leaving the family by the nature of the labor market. Although some women have always had to work and others worked either before marriage or when their husbands died, society did not encourage women to work. No laws required equal pay for equal work or prohibited discrimination in hiring or promotion. Women were expected to stay home and take care of husband and children. Under some circumstances, a married woman who rejected her wifely role was considered at fault because, in effect, in doing so she abandoned her family; her husband could divorce her without paying alimony and in some cases was awarded custody of the children.

Much of the old consensus was rooted in brute economic reality. There were not enough jobs in the cash-income-producing economy to employ many women. Thirty years ago ours was a manufacturing society, not an information-processing and service society. Although today women can work as coal miners by using sophisticated equipment, in the 1950s there were few women who could load fifteen tons of coal a day by hand, and fewer who wanted to. Agriculture was the exception, and women worked long hours to produce cash crops on family farms.

It is only since the 1960s that millions of jobs have opened up requiring either light physical work, intelligence, or organizational skill rather than raw strength and stamina. The old consensus was predicated on the need to support women who could not find work other than homemaking. Yesteryear's division of labor was not entirely arbitrary or irrational: men worked in commerce, manufacturing, and services that produced cash income; women worked in child-rearing and domestic occupations that produced comfort and enhanced the quality of life. It took our grandmothers four times as long to do the cooking, cleaning, and laundry in an age without electrical appliances, frozen foods, and permanent press clothes as it takes a modern homemaker.

Certainly the days of the old consensus were not a golden age that beckons our swift return. There was widespread slavery of a sort for both men and women. However, the old consensus must be taken into account in any analysis of contemporary divorce courts because much of today's divorce law was formulated at that time. Many people, in fact, are still proponents of the old consensus, and some of them are judges. More to the point is the simple fact that most couples over forty entered into marriage under the rules of the old consensus, so that recent changes in those rules often defeat their legitimate expectations, which in turn leads to justified disparagement of the justice dished out by domestic courts.

There are three distinct generations of potential customers for the domestic courts: couples in their early twenties who have been married a short time and have no children; couples in their late twenties, thirties, and forties who have been married for a number of years and have children of varying ages; and couples in their fifties and sixties who have been married as long as thirty to forty years and have grown children and, often, grandchildren. While not everyone in a given age group fits his or her generation's profile, nonetheless these basic profiles are important to an understanding of what courts are doing.

No single set of rules can be fairly applied to every divorcing couple because couples' problems are different. Some of these differences relate to their generational profile; others relate only to the background, work experience, and personalities of the people involved. To a greater extent than in any other area of the law, the domestic relations judge is allowed broad discretion to achieve a fair result on an individual, case-by-case basis. The amount of alimony and child support, the custody of the children, the extent of visitation rights, and the use or division of property acquired during the marriage are all "within the sound discretion of the trial court judge," as appellate courts are fond of pointing out.

Most of the state statutes governing domestic matters give only vague instructions to the judges, which means that it is difficult to predict what judges will do in any particular case. Appellate courts attempt to set some uniform standards and often reverse outrageous rulings by trial court judges, but when they do, they almost always say that there was an "abuse of discretion." Even in appellate courts the decisions in domestic cases tend to be ad hoc; the rules are not sufficiently specific in many areas (e.g.,

9

child custody and property awards) to assure accurate predictions of what a court will do.

The fading consensus about the role of marriage and, therefore, about the rules that govern marriage, make it difficult for courts to achieve results that appear just in everyone's eyes. In addition to differences that relate to the age of the couple, the age of their children, and the length of their marriage, there are differences relating to socioeconomic status, education, religion, and geographical area. For example, women whose primary work opportunities are in factories or in clerical work are less enthusiastic about women's liberation and the work outside the home that liberation entails than are women who have recently graduated from the Harvard Business School.

The only group that presents few problems to the courts with respect to reconciling economic and emotional interests are young, childless couples. By and large, these people can be married and divorced with few consequences more untoward than those that would arise if they had been living together and just split up. Alimony is not an issue, except in extraordinary circumstances, and the most difficult question a court is liable to be called on to decide is the division of personal property. It is a tragedy, however, when rules formulated with this group in mind are then applied to other groups with different problems.

Couples now over forty-five all entered into marriage when the old consensus was a vital force. Depending upon a woman's socioeconomic background and her aspirations, she frequently married right out of high school or after one or two years of college. Since opportunities for women were limited in higher-paying supervisory, executive, or professional jobs, women were encouraged by almost all social institutions to regard an advantageous marriage as the best path to economic security and a fulfilling life. Such job training as these women had was rudimentary—they usually did factory or office work requiring only entry-level skills. They generally instead developed and refined home-making and child care skills, which were highly regarded when their generation was young but which have little market value. These women expected marriage and family to be their careers.

Men now over forty-five had similar expectations. They expected their wives to be good homemakers, attentive mothers, and, often, devoted servants as well. If the men had management jobs, they expected their wives to accompany them to business-related social functions and to entertain associates. Coal miners expected their wives to prepare elaborate dinners to be eaten several miles underground and to wash clothes that would give nightmares to the advertising agency that makes Tide commercials. Men in the Armed Forces and the construction trades expected wives to be good sports about their being away for weeks, months, or even years at a time; and all ambitious men expected their wives to pull up stakes without complaint at opportunity's summons.

While this is only an impressionistic outline that fails to take into account the subtleties of millions of individual marriages, it has value as a generalization. Marriage under the old consensus was a particular type of economic partnership. Marriage among young people today is still an economic partnership but is one of a different type. When an older couple divorces, the domestic court must do justice to the parties according to the rules that they thought would apply to them—not according to new rules that they never contemplated and for which they are unprepared. Men and women over forty have foreclosed many options because of the old rules; and there is no going back.

Middle-class women who married twenty-five years ago did not expect to return to the labor force full time unless they became widows. Responsible men who could afford it made sure that there was insurance for such an eventuality. While a good many women over forty-five have taken part-time jobs to supplement the family income or to fill their idle hours, few of them are prepared to be their own sole support; most do not possess skills that can be marketed at a rate that would sustain their lifestyles. In the job market their age is against them, notwithstanding statutes prohibiting age discrimination, and they may not be sufficiently flexible to adjust to the demands of office or factory work.

Some older women, of course, are more employable than others. Nurses can always reenter the labor market, as can skilled secretaries, real estate salespersons, and, in places where the market is not glutted, teachers. But the fact that some older women can make a smooth transition from homemaker to employed worker does not mean that all women can do so. Nor does it mean that a nurse can sustain the same standard of living on a salary of $16,000 a year that she had while married to a successful dentist.

There is very little quarrel with an award of alimony to a woman who has devoted her entire adult life to homemaking if the husband is at fault in the breakup of the home. He may become physically or psychologically brutal, or he may take up with other women and abandon or at least disgrace his wife. But what if the woman is outrageously unpleasant and drives him to act in such ways? Who is at fault then? A further wrinkle to the problem is that it is far easier to prove that a man is a wife beater or an adulterer than to prove that a woman is so unpleasant as to have forced a breakup.

Often middle-aged couples just decide that they do not want to stay married. In such a situation neither party is more at fault than the other, but there is more to divorce than just bidding each other farewell. The economic consequences of divorce are different for a middle-aged man than for a middle-aged woman. The man has a position in the market economy, while the woman usually does not. Assets acquired during the marriage are likely to be in the man's name, even though such assets were acquired through joint efforts. A woman in her late forties has less attractive prospects for a second marriage than a man of comparable age, and since women live longer than men, there are more single, middle-aged women than single, middle-aged men. Finally, a woman is unlikely to have any vested pension rights other than Social Security, which will be miserly unless she secures ten years of high-wage work. Her situation is similar to that of a worker who leaves an industry because his or her plant closes; but in these circumstances a good union would see that he or she is awarded severance pay, retrained, and, if possible, reemployed.

One of the major changes in divorce laws over the last fifteen years is that most states now permit "no-fault" divorces. In some places such divorces still require one or two years of voluntary separation, but elsewhere a mere petition to the court asking for dissolution of the marriage because of "irreconcilable differences" suffices. Fault and no-fault divorces each have different legal implications. For example, no-fault divorces are usually consensual, and the consensual nature of the proceeding often facilitates agreements on child custody, support, distribution of property, and even alimony.

On occasion, however, the parties proceeding under no-fault can agree only that they want a divorce but must ask a court to settle the other matters. At that point the court is directed by the statutes to establish fair and equitable terms for the dissolution of the marriage. One important inquiry that a court has to pursue in making a fair award is whether one party behaved badly (inequitably) toward the other. Bad behavior, or "inequitable conduct," amounts to something less than the serious fault that would in and of itself justify a divorce, but it nonetheless causes the greater part of the blame for the dissolution of the marriage to fall on one party.

Under no-fault, a domestic court has the power to make a just award of personal property and alimony without finding either party at fault. A middle-aged wife may get alimony because of the economics of her circumstances, not necessarily because she has been wronged. Yet a trial court judge is not required to award alimony, and many considerations may prevent a woman from receiving it. If she has job skills or has been working, she will receive less money; if her children are grown, she will get less than if she still has young children at home; and if the judge is unsympathetic to women, she may not receive anything.

On the other hand, if the trial judge is sympathetic to women, he or she may give a middle-aged wife a large alimony award, and the husband may feel unfairly put upon. Where a wife complains that she is being stifled by her homemaking role and decides to enter the labor market to relieve her boredom or to have income of her own, the husband's expectations may be confounded. Although the

14

wife is not technically at fault—she has not committed adultery, become an alcoholic, or been excessively abusive —she has still violated the terms of partnership implicit at the time of marriage. This fact does not, however, change her unfavorable economic circumstances.

WHEN we turn our attention to couples who have been married for several years and have young children at home, a host of new considerations enters the picture. We are no longer concerned exclusively with doing justice between husband and wife; we are concerned as well with the best interests of the children. Often justice for the children inhibits justice between the husband and wife, and the courts are in a quandary trying to figure out for whom they are expected to do justice. At the most basic level, it is often against the best interests of the children to award them to the blameless spouse.

Although lifestyles are rapidly changing, particularly in the higher socioeconomic groups, women are still usually responsible for child care. Mothers on average spend at least three times as many hours with young children every day as do fathers; as a result, the children have stronger bonds with the mother and a higher level of dependence on her. Also, the demands of male work make it comparatively more difficult for fathers to be competent single-parent caretakers of young children even if they have the support of baby-sitters, relatives, or day-care centers. Lawyers, doctors, traveling salesmen, construction trades workers, coal miners on the midnight shift, and others with long or irregular hours or with jobs that require travel have a hard time being single parents.

Yet, while children may not be as deeply attached to

their fathers as they are to their mothers, fathers are often deeply attached to their children. When a family breaks up exclusively as the result of a wife's misconduct or because of her unilateral decision to quit the marriage, the husband feels unjustly punished if he loses his children. Numerous women have run off with other men in the face of a husband's extraordinary efforts to preserve the marriage, and yet the court has felt compelled to give custody of the children to the mother. When I have made such decisions, I have been overwhelmed by a sense of sorrow. Where this result is required, the decision is obviously outrageous from the father's perspective. But what if the father is not as good a parent as the mother? In such a case, awarding custody to the father is outrageous from the children's perspective.

Under the old consensus the rules surrounding custody awards were very confusing. Supposedly, custody was awarded in the best interests of the children, but misconduct, particularly sexual misconduct, on the part of the wife tended to prove that she was an "unfit" parent, in which case the father got the children. The same rule applied to the father, of course, but the problem was academic because a blameless wife almost always got the children anyway. Since judges, too, have been influenced by sexual liberation and women's liberation, judge-made divorce law increasingly ignores most sexual misconduct on the part of a woman in determining the award of custody.

As strict standards of sexual morality are increasingly rejected, a divorced woman's living with a man does not necessarily imply unfitness to rear children; likewise, a woman's having had an affair before divorce is thought to have little bearing on her capacity to care for children. Some states, such as West Virginia, have adopted these views. Regardless of the published rules, however, trial court judges are notorious for manipulating them to achieve results that coincide with their own definitions of morality.

Economics alone dictates that even a blameless husband support his children. At the same time, the best interests of the children frequently require that they be awarded to their mother even when she was responsible for the breakup of the marriage. This means that a father can be saddled with supporting children whom he never sees and who may even have been turned against him. A blameless father often emerges from divorce court with all the financial reponsibility of marriage and none of its emotional or economic rewards. Everyone else in the game has received justice, and he is understandably enraged. In recent years this justified sense of rage has led to the formation of militant men's lobbying groups that seek divorce laws more favorable to fathers.

The blameless wife, however, fares little better—in fact, most of the time she does worse. In the first instance, her husband can intimidate her into an unjust compromise on the matters of alimony and child support by threatening her with a custody battle. Although in most places the mother would probably win, almost all states now have either statutes or judge-made law that forbids an explicit maternal preference. This sex-neutral rule seemingly requires exhaustive inquiry into the relative fitness of both parents if the custody question is contested. If the wife is deeply attached to her children, as most mothers are, she is likely to be unwilling to take a chance on the courtroom roulette wheel no matter how favorable the odds, and she will therefore agree to accept less money than she is entitled to in return for no challenge to her custody rights.

The mistreated wife has the worst of all possible worlds:

she is saddled with caring for young children, which obviously circumscribes her social life and opportunities to find a new husband, and she must enter the labor force to make up the difference between what she receives from her former husband and what it costs her to live and support the children. If her former husband is not tied by either his job or kinship to the geographical area where she is living, he can flee to distant parts, in which case she might as well whistle "Dixie" as try to enforce her alimony and child support awards.

It is expensive to prosecute a former husband who is reluctant to pay his support money. Although the states, and recently the federal government, give some assistance, the number of government personnel available to help a woman get support money is woefully inadequate. In any event, even with government help, the effectiveness of enforcement is in inverse relation to both the mobility and the income of the defaulting man. Where a man moves frequently or does not earn much money, the woman has little hope of receiving sustained support. The sad fact of divorce law is that the wicked tend to prosper and the innocent to suffer in spite of the best efforts of the courts.

It is often thought that divorce courts carefully scrutinize the issue of fault or inequitable conduct and attempt to make alimony and child custody awards that reflect relative degrees of bad behavior. In my experience, lip service is more or less paid to such a theory, but in practice the blame principle cannot be applied in any but the most clear-cut cases. Blame was taken into consideration thirty years ago to a far greater extent that it is today because under the old consensus society could agree on what was blameworthy. It was expected that a woman would move if her husband was transferred or got a better job elsewhere. He was the primary breadwinner, and the wife's career had no bearing on her moral and hence legal obligation to follow him to brighter economic opportunities. Few young people today would agree that such a rule is an acceptable legal principle.

In a two-career family, who is going to move and for what reason are subjects for continual negotiation. When these negotiations reach an impasse, who is at fault? Certainly a court cannot tell you. Similarly, adultery used to be considered substantial fault. It still has many of the same consequences for a man, but a woman will usually not lose her children as a result of restrained extramarital sexual behavior. Only if her conduct is so outrageous as to imply that she is an unfit mother will she forfeit her children. Although she is not entitled to alimony if she has committed adultery, how is she to take care of the children if she is starving to death? Inevitably, the child support award must be generous enough to subsidize her own living expenses.

Family relationships tend to arouse our most intense emotions. When a family breaks up other than by mutual agreement, the parties are often seeking not just a settlement of their legal entitlements; they are also seeking to punish their spouse or even their children for years of what they perceive as accumulated wrongs. Immature domestic litigants expect the court to award moral victories by the way they decide child custody, support, alimony, and property matters.

In the same way, however, that a domestic court is unable to provide a viable alternative to the economies and emotional support provided by marriage, it also has difficulty vindicating moral positions. A woman in her late fifties may be impossible to live with, but it is a disproportionate punishment to cast her out on the street without alimony after she has spent thirty years as a housewife. In a similar spirit, even a brutal and adulterous man cannot be forced to give all his income to a blameless wife, since he must be able to live too. If alimony and support payments are confiscatory, the man either flees or stops working.

The application of a blame theory is also impaled on another practical problem. More often than not, the equities in any marriage are not as clear-cut to an impartial observer as they appear to the parties involved. The woman who becomes outrageously unpleasant may have been driven to it by the sexual indifference and boorishness of her husband. The husband who consorts with other women or becomes violent often does so because of his wife's nagging and lack of affection. Even when one party is almost entirely at fault and the other is almost entirely blameless, it is difficult to demonstrate that to a court against all the background noise that any contested case naturally stimulates.

For example, my wife and I are happily married. We accept each other's eccentricities with a cheerful equanimity and write off whatever annoyance they cause us by dwelling on each other's good qualities. However, the situation would be reversed were we to enter court for a contested divorce. Suddenly my late hours, frequent travel, devotion of most weekends to writing, my intemperate language, and eccentric approaches to education would assume enormous proportions. Similarly, my wife's indifference to the use of her Visa card, lack of compulsion in housekeeping, and willingness to convert the entire house into a nursery could be shown to have produced great mental anguish in me. Each of us could hire doctors as experts to testify about how the conduct of the other undermined our health and well-being; friends and relatives could relate particularly abusive episodes that they had observed. The poor judge would need to decide who was more at fault than the other. (Inevitably, he or she would decide that we were both crazy and deserved each other.)

Adultery, alcoholism, drug addiction, incurable insanity, and physical brutality are usually set out by statute as grounds for a fault divorce. When any of these grounds has been established with respect to one party, a court must find that party at fault. However, the ground for divorce known in most places as "mental cruelty" or "cruel and inhuman treatment" is an open-ended rascal. Where one party thinks that he or she has the goods on the other because of adultery or physical brutality, the other party can countersue on the ground of mental cruelty. In most states, if both parties are at fault, neither is entitled to a divorce on a fault ground. (This rule, in fact, often converts a fault-based divorce into a no-fault divorce.) When a classic fault ground such as drug abuse is countered by an allegation of mental cruelty, the court must decide how people have treated each other over the years. Asking a judge to make such a decision on the basis of courtroom testimony is like asking a doctor to do brain surgery with a meat ax. Certain limitations are inherent in the tools available to a judge.

The problem in applying any theory of fault or inequitable conduct is that a judge must sort out what has taken place during many years of married life. Each party can tell his or her side of the story, and each can bring witnesses. Different people respond to others' behavior in different ways. Some men are happy with a fussy, nagging wife—

they accept her nagging as evidence that she cares; other men find such a companion unbearable. Some women will not tolerate the least physical abuse—one slap and they leave forever; other women accept a certain amount of physical coercion as evidence of a robust, even passionate relationship.[1]

A divorce court judge with a nagging wife may find the accusation of nagging less persuasive than would another judge. Similarly, a woman judge with an abhorrence of physical violence may be more outraged by a man's physical brutality than is warranted under the circumstances of a particular relationship. On the other hand, even a woman judge—if she was reared in an environment where moderate physical displays of emotion toward husbands, wives, and children were commonplace and accepted—may not understand the seriousness to some women of mild physical abuse or their abhorrence of corporal punishment of children.

Most of the testimony in divorce proceedings is gibberish. Witnesses relate isolated incidents of misconduct and often focus on activity that the judge considers inconsequential. In one recent child custody fight in my court, one hundred pages of the record involved testimony about whether the parents smoked marijuana, which parent smoked more, and under what circumstances they smoked.

---

1. In a recent case before my court there was a couple who routinely attacked each other with knives and shotguns in the general direction of the other while engaged in all-night drinking bouts. The Department of Welfare tried to take their children, and they both appeared in court to defend themselves on the ground that they were careful never to discharge guns when the children were around. While the litigation was in progress, they grabbed the children and fled to Florida, where they are apparently happily drinking and brawling. The unbeliever may read the story in *Department of Welfare* v. *Keesee,* 297 S.E. 2d 200 (W.Va. 1982).

Well, in a certain age group almost everyone smokes mari-juana occasionally; if divorce courts awarded children only to people who never smoked marijuana, the state departments of welfare would be flooded with wards of the state. The litigants spent a full day on a subject that I, as a judge, find irrelevant. Domestic courts pretend to do something that they cannot do—namely, sort out what went wrong with a marriage and award benefits and punishments in keeping with relative degrees of fault. Although there are some clear-cut cases of fault on only one side, these are usually not the cases that are litigated.

But the question of who was at fault in the marriage is comparatively simple in comparison to the knotty question of which parent should have custody of children. When the parties in a divorce have enough money, they can hire psychiatrists, psychologists, social workers, and educators who will testify to anything. The opinions of such experts are based on interviews with the parents and children and occasionally on some standard tests. Unless these professionals have been involved with the parents and children over a substantial period for reasons unrelated to their employment as expert witnesses, their testimony is valueless —it is witch doctory at best and perjury at worst. Judges listen to it because that's the game, but it is a rare judge who lets expert opinion override his or her common sense. If he or she did, the side with the money to hire the most or the best experts would always have the advantage.

A lot of factors can rightfully go into a determination of custody. The most important concern is which parent has the strongest bond with the children. Occasionally one parent will be obviously unfit—he or she will fail to feed, clothe, supervise, or protect the child. But that is comparatively rare. Usually both parents are fit, and the question is which parent is the more capable. An initial decision on this subject, however, is not final.

Many of the most intractable child custody problems arise after the person awarded custody remarries; decides upon a new, demanding career; or takes on a live-in housemate of the opposite sex. (Gay parents present a whole new set of considerations.) Obviously, a court cannot foresee these problems at the time of divorce and the initial custody award. Taking care of a child may be a eighteen-year project. If a person wants to make child custody litigation a lifetime hobby, he or she can come back into court anytime he or she can allege any "change of circumstances."

Where both parents are fit, the court usually awards young children to the mother initially, merely because she is likely to know more about child care than her husband and be closer to the children. While often, in fact, the father would be the better caretaker, there is no practicable way to prove that. Since demonstrating which of two fit parents will be the better custodian is almost impossible to do, judges resort to rules of thumb like "maternal preference," relying only on statistical average because the statistical average may very well be the most, not the least, reliable evidence.

When children are older and can formulate an intelligent opinion about their own custody, they are frequently called as witnesses. However, in protracted custody cases this can lead to competitive bribery of the children. The parent who acts responsibly and refuses to engage in such practices often finds himself or herself the object of negative testimony by the children and can lose custody because he or she was actually the better parent.

In some domestic cases correct results in terms of moral vindication are inevitably at odds with acceptable economic results. Because in the ordinary case domestic courts cannot focus on right and wrong within a marriage, the inescapable conclusion is that domestic courts are in business primarily to solve economic, not emotional, problems. Women, therefore, appear to emerge from domestic court with more of what they came for than men do. Hence the well-known country song alleging that she got the gold mine and he got the shaft.

However, if we leave aside divorces among wealthy professionals and the superrich, women usually achieve only a pyrrhic victory. The 1980 census demonstrates that women as a class are much poorer than men. Women earn lower wages, and their work tends to be less secure. Among all persons entitled to private retirement benefits in 1978 the median entitlement for men was $2,080; for women it was $970.

The controversy that has surrounded women's liberation, men's liberation, and sexual liberation has distracted us from the harsh economic consequences that attend the breakdown of the family. The mere fact that the voices of professionally trained, upper-middle-class women are resonant does not imply that they speak for a majority. Although a woman without graduate school training *can* hold relatively high paying jobs, such as police officer, coal mine foreman, machinery salesperson, or automobile dealer, for whatever reason, not very many women actually secure such jobs.

In fact, a whole new class of poor is emerging in America—untrained divorced women with minor children. Women, who constitute 42 percent of the work force nationwide, are concentrated in a small number of occupations, with low pay and limited opportunities. Government studies show that in 1981, half of the 43 million women in the labor force were employed in only twenty occupations: secretary, bookkeeper, salesclerk retail worker, cashier, waitress, registered nurse, elementary school teacher, private household worker, typist, nursing aide, sewer and stitcher, cook, receptionist, secondary school teacher, assembler, bank teller, building interior cleaner, hairdresser, cleaner and servant, and child care worker.

There is strong evidence that occupational segregation of women is increasing. In 1950, 62 percent of all clerical workers were women; by 1978 the figure had risen to 79 percent. Even if a woman with young children does get a job, her career opportunities are circumscribed because she must return home promptly each evening, and she loses workdays when the children are ill. Jobs that require frequent travel or extensive overtime are almost entirely foreclosed. Although highly paid professional women can combine child custody with demanding work, their flexibility is directly related to sufficient income to hire a full-time, competent surrogate parent. If a woman is a barber, a secretary, or a factory worker, such an arrangement is impossible.

A woman, therefore, does not win anything of economic value when she gets custody of her children. Indeed, she loses the opportunity to exploit fully her abilities in the labor market or to return to school. Consequently, even if a woman is largely at fault in the breakup of a marriage, domestic court judges may bend the rules to award her alimony. In 1978, however, only 14 percent of all divorced women were awarded any alimony. Furthermore, of the women who were awarded alimony, only two-thirds of them received any actual payment, and the median payment for those who received it was only $2,850 a year. Alimony and child support payments are likely to be the bills that get paid last. If the television goes on the blink, the serviceman will be paid in cash, but many divorced wives must fight every month of their lives for their checks. By the time a woman has finished rearing the children, many opportunities will have passed her by, and she will need some continuing help unless she remarries.

Under the old consensus many of these problems were eliminated. When older people found that they did not enjoy living together, they remained married but went their separate ways. Thus, they preserved pension rights, the economies of joint households, and interests in spouses' estates. Men often consorted with other women with their wives' acquiescence, and the women followed their own interests. It was not a perfect or even a desirable arrangement, but it did avoid the economic problems for older women that are presented by today's divorce-prone society.

When, therefore, divorce courts appear not to render justice, it is because each of us has a subjective standard by which we define "justice." Certainly courts cannot give moral vindication to one party at the expense of the economic well-being of the other parties involved. When the courts are accused of being overly generous to women and failing to take the legitimate grievances of men seriously, it is forgotten that the new class of poor women and poor children is becoming a social problem of major proportions.

Finally, judges are human, and their decisions are influenced by their backgrounds, experiences, and—unfortunately—prejudices. Unlike other areas of the law where general rules can be crafted by legislatures or multimember appellate courts, domestic relations cases do not lend themselves to concrete rules. The most important consideration in a domestic case is not the law that applies but the facts of the marriage and the circumstances of the parties. Conclusions about these factual questions must be left largely within the discretion of trial judges who hear the testimony, observe the live witnesses, and get some sense of the personalities involved. Although justice is on balance better served by allowing wide discretion than by imposing any tightly crafted scheme of ironclad rules, inevitably where there is room for discretion, there is also room for caprice.

2
Abstracting Life into Law

THE process for making decisions in divorce cases reminds me of an episode that occurred when I was a soldier. One day I was sent with a team of officers to a remote Vietnamese village to pay war damage claims. These payments were governed by the Military Assistance Command Vietnam (MACV). When I arrived at the village, I found that none of the senior American officers had a copy of the original MACV regulations. A Vietnamese officer, however, had a copy of the regulations that had been translated from English into Vietnamese, but no American officer spoke Vietnamese. The Vietnamese didn't speak English, but he and I both spoke French, so he translated the Vietnamese version of the regulations into French. I then retranslated them into English. Needless to say, what emerged bore little resemblance to the original English version.

Any contested divorce case involves a similar process of translation and retranslation. The judge wants to understand what went on during the marriage, yet he or she is constrained to understand it through the clouded glass of successive and imperfect translations.

The first translation occurs when the lawyers choose the facts they consider important and the evidence they think will prove those facts. Surveying the lives of their clients, they select discrete episodes that fit into such preconceived legal pigeonholes as adultery, abandonment, or mental cruelty and that are expected to trigger favorable responses from the court. The court puts up with this artificial sorting process because the complex and fluid lives of the parties must somehow be reduced to manageable proportions. Any other scheme would be disorderly, by court standards. That abstraction and organization are necessary does not, of course, eliminate the problem of inaccurate translation.

The second translation occurs when the witnesses chosen to present the facts testify. Some witnesses are perceptive and articulate and others are not; some are sensitive to emotional nuances and others are not; some immediately generate goodwill with the court and others arouse hostility; some lie and others tell the truth. Whether the stories that emerge from the mouths of the witnesses disappoint or please the lawyer, each is likely to tell a tale at least slightly different from the other and also from the one the lawyer had in mind.

The last level of translation occurs when the court decides what to do on decreeing a divorce. The best solution that a court can envisage can seldom be incorporated into an enforceable decree. For example, a court can award custody of a child to one party and reasonable visitation rights to the other party, but cannot prevent the parties from disparaging each other to the child or bickering about visitation. The court can make a distribution of the property acquired during the marriage and award alimony, but it cannot usually rearrange insurance policies, pension rights, or entitlements under Social Security.

Many people regularly resolve controversies. Parents resolve quarrels among children; principals resolve disputes among teachers; supervisors resolve differences among workers; labor arbitrators resolve issues between unions and management. What distinguishes courts from other individuals or institutions is their procedure. All judges, including domestic judges, must obtain their information about a case through a formal adversary process where relevant information is presented by the parties. Unlike parents, school principals, supervisors, or labor arbitrators, however, judges have no prior knowledge of the parties before them. Judges do not make independent investigations; nor do they control the scope of the issues that are brought to them for decision. The litigants, through their lawyers, present the entire case to the judge in two packages. Each litigant determines the theory of law that seems most likely to produce favorable results, the evidence needed to prove that theory, and the defenses available to counter the other side's theory. Each then attempts to sell its package to the judge.

Court procedures alienate most domestic litigants because emotion-charged human problems must be presented exclusively in terms of preexisting, abstract legal categories. Litigants are disappointed that they are not permitted to spill their guts. For example, if a couple is divorcing because of fights over money, both must characterize what each did to the other as "cruel and inhuman treatment." If their problem stems from a poor sexual relationship, they must present this problem as either cruelty or adultery. Emotional satisfactions are often denied when complex personal relationships must be dissected so that the parts can be forced into one or another preconceived legal category.

31

Litigant satisfaction in divorce matters is far lower than in any other type of case. Most judges who are murdered by dissatisfied customers are killed by irate domestic litigants, not by criminals. The reason is simple: in other litigation, fewer emotional issues are involved; more important, the judge has less discretion. His or her personal philosophy and prejudices intrude themselves less forcefully into decisions. In other lawsuits it is not necessary to understand the entire life history of the parties to reach correct results. For example, if a lawsuit is about a personal injury, the court need focus only on the events surrounding that injury—often a period of no more than several seconds.

When the emotional makeup and total life history of the litigants are immaterial to deciding a case, the adversary system with its demand for legal abstraction works reasonably well. In domestic cases, however, where a court must be informed about long histories of complex relationships among spouses, children, in-laws, and collateral relatives, the formal adversary system is an unrefined tool for generating all the appropriate information. Furthermore, the judge must decide what conduct is blameworthy, the relative degrees of blame, and the relation of blame to such issues as property division, alimony, and child custody. Obviously, whenever an issue like blame must be decided, the invitation to subjectivity is open-ended.

Outside domestic law, most civil lawsuits are about money. The law of injuries to people and property, called "torts," is about making the party who causes damage pay for that damage; the law of contracts is about enforcing agreements that arise in business; the law of property is about who owns what. The common denominator elsewhere in civil law is a perceived, and generally definite, economic loss. It is, therefore, often possible to simplify the issues in a case to whether there was a loss, who caused that loss, and whether the person who caused the loss is legally bound to make it good. In deciding these types of issues there is little or no invitation to judicial subjectivity, and as often as not the party who must pay the money is an insurance company whose very business it is to pay money.

In addition to subjectivity, we must consider the depth of judicial intrusion. In the run-of-mine civil suit what is relevant and what is not are quite clear—inquiry into the alleged homosexuality of an accident victim, for instance, will not be permitted. The trial concerns itself with specific events concentrated in a specific time frame, and with only certain relevant aspects of these events. A family court must consider as best it can the entire family life of the parties, determine as best it can who has been a good or bad parent or spouse, and divide up the proceeds. Where a defeated plantiff in a fender-bender case may grudgingly be willing to admit that he or she may after all have been negligent, an inquiry of vast scope into matters of personal importance will not be viewed so philosophically. Whereas parties to a civil suit generally seek recovery, parties who come before a family court are often seeking redemption. After all the evidence and legal arguments have been presented, the judge must attempt to reconstruct in his or her mind what actually happened in real-life, human terms over the years. To make matters worse, even though a good judge will base his or her decision on a grasp of human interaction, he or she must then explain that decision in terms of abstract legal principles so that the case can be processed through the machinery of an appellate court. It should not surprise us that when this process is finally over the decisions are often incomprehensible to the parties involved and those acquainted with them. Little wonder that domestic judges are murdered more often than other types of judges are.

The unique element of domestic law is that the events triggering a divorce are subjective to the couple involved. Some other types of cases, such as libel and slander suits, fights over boundaries by neighbors, and right-of-way disputes, can also be characterized by subjective considerations of spite and personal animosity, but there is always some objective standard to which the parties may be held. In any event, these cases are comparatively rare; most civil cases involve money, purely and simply. When maximization of economic gain is what litigants want it is easy to develop predictable general rules that will encourage people to settle their differences out of court.

When the issue is money, a litigant must weigh the cost of litigation, the likelihood of winning, and the delay in receiving payment that litigation entails against available opportunities for quick settlement. After weighing these factors, he or she will usually adopt the most profitable course of action. Irate and hardheaded businesspersons will settle cases on the advice of their lawyers if going to court will cost more than settlement. Not so for divorce clients; the emotionally scarred often use a courtroom confrontation for purposes unrelated to the value of the ultimate judicial award.

Domestic law is so subjective and unpredictable because the complexity of legal structures faithfully reflects the complexity of the subject matter that the legal structure is attempting to regulate. Family life in a society like ours where job roles, the geographical location of economic opportunities, and the community sense of morality are in constant flux is a confusing creature to regulate. In this regard, it might be useful to compare for a moment our murder law with our domestic law.

The law of murder has well-defined rules. In order for a murder to be committed, someone must have killed someone else. Once it is demonstrated that one person intentionally killed another, the only question remaining is whether the killing was justified in whole or in part. Self-defense justifies killing entirely. Heat of passion, such as occurs on finding one's spouse in bed with a lover, justifies killing in part—it will usually reduce the charge of murder to voluntary manslaughter. Insanity, if proved, exculpates altogether because it removes the elements of malice and intent.

There is little complaint about how the courts handle murder cases. Complaints that we do hear almost always concern either freeing the guilty because the police blundered or sentences that are not sufficiently severe. The rules surrounding a murder prosecution itself are tight and predictable, reflecting the simplicity of the subject matter and the small set of possible considerations that must engage a court's attention. Furthermore, the structure's simplicity encourages most murderers to plead guilty in return for some sentence reduction rather than go to trial. In a murder case everyone can predict with almost exact certainty what will happen in court if the case goes to jury trial.

In comparison to murder, domestic relations are vastly more complex and loosely defined. The permutations of emotional, social, and economic interactions among married persons and their children during a marriage are limitless. In a murder prosecution the only questions to be answered are : (1) Did someone get killed? (2) Who did the killing? and (3) Is the killer excused in whole or in part? In a domestic case, on the other hand, the court must explore the economic circumstances of the parties, their prospects for future livelihoods, the relationships of the children with the parents, the way husband and wife treated each other throughout the marriage, who was at fault in the breakup of the marriage, who contributed how much and under what conditions to the assets accumulated during the course of the marriage, and what custody arrangement is in the best interests of the children.

Unlike a prosecution for murder, there is no logical sequence for deciding the issues in a domestic case; also unlike a murder prosecution, resolution of one issue does not automatically foreclose inquiry into others. A wife can be at fault in the breakup of the home yet nonetheless be the better parent for custody of the children; a husband may be brutal and overbearing, but the wife may be in a superior economic position and, therefore, not entitled to alimony or child support. (In fact, in some states, particularly the community-property states, the husband might be entitled to part of the wife's property.) Neither parent may want the children, and the decision about custody may ultimately concern the fitness of grandparents, collateral relatives, or even friends. If property has been acquired during the marriage, the court must make some distribution of it to each party; and this distribution, depending on the state, may or may not be influenced by the conduct of the parties during the marriage.

The law governing murder is fairly simple because there

is no sentiment in favor of taking economic and social factors into account. The poor are not entitled to kill the rich; the smart cannot kill the stupid; whites cannot kill blacks; and spurned lovers cannot kill the objects of their love. Since the object of murder law is to accomplish a simple result—prevent unjustified killing—the mechanics of enforcement can be uncomplicated.

Thus we see that complexity per se is not necessarily an inherent part of lawsuits. When there is general agreement in a society about how human affairs in a particular area should be regulated, the rules can be uncomplicated. The complexity of our domestic law is directly related both to the complexity of economic and social arrangements in the modern American family and to the lack of consensus about rights and obligations in that family. Domestic law is not necessarily complex, as a look at any primitive society quickly discloses.

Outside the Western industrialized nations, divorce rates are comparatively low. In nonindustrial societies the options available for feeding, housing, clothing, and nurturing women and children outside a family setting are limited. Because there is a consensus in most poorer societies that the family unit must be preserved to meet much of the population's basic needs, the laws governing divorce can be simple and appear just to the members of those societies. And indeed the divorce laws of primitive countries look very much like our murder laws. Families are expected to stay together, so there is no room for nuance in the legal structure's analysis of reasons for breaking up. Often the most serious grounds for divorce, such as adultery, are punished as criminal offenses—occasionally, as in Saudi Arabia, with death. Where the goals of the family are economic rather than emotional or romantic, the legal structure reflects the comparative simplicity of achieving these goals.

The most important qualities that all law, including domestic law, must have are fair general rules, predictability, and some system to protect us from the idiot judge. Unfortunately, these qualities are at odds with one another, and nowhere in the law is this circumstance more obvious than in domestic matters.

King Solomon is held up as the paradigm of the just judge. When two women were fighting over a child, Solomon ordered the child cut in half in the justified expectation that the real mother would abandon her claim rather than see her child murdered. The advantage that Solomon had over modern judges was that he could make up law as he went along. He was not circumscribed either by statutes or by precedent. His only concern was what was fair to the parties and society in each individual case. Such an approach has obvious drawbacks, not the least of which is its lack of predictability. Yet if Solomon's technique had been predictable, it would not have worked, since the litigants would have calculated their responses. Further, what happens when Solomon's idiot son eventually succeeds him?

The fairer the law attempts to be, or the greater the extent to which judges can take all the litigants' real-life problems into consideration, the less predictable law becomes. When, for example, a bank holds a mortgage and the underlying debt is not paid, the bank expects the mortgaged property to be sold to satisfy its claim. If a court could consider that the person who owes the money is a widow with three children who will be put out on the street when the bank forecloses, the bank knows in advance that only an unusual court would enforce the bank's claim against the widow. Banks would then avoid loans to widows.

Business requires that the law be predictable. For the law to be predictable, all life must be abstracted into preconceived legal categories. Thus, if any person borrows money, he or she must pay it back or lose his or her property—it makes no difference whether the person is a Rockefeller or the destitute widow Brown. All the individual's particular circumstances must be ignored in favor of the abstract legal category of "debtor." This process of abstraction, although highly suitable to the resolution of simple disputes about money, leaves much to be desired when applied to the resolution of complex emotional matters. Businesspersons predicate their day-to-day dealings on their understanding of the law. Few husbands and wives, on the other hand, give a moment's thought to their legal rights until divorce is imminent. Most people are optimists; in fact, given current statistics on divorce, marriage is probably the greatest exercise in optimism that most people experience. In 1984 the odds are against any couple making it for life, but people don't think about odds when they are in love, passionately attracted sexually, or lonely.

Losers in lawsuits usually attribute their defeat to the benighted nature of the judge rather than to the strength of the other side's case, which means that hardly any judge, regardless of his or her ability, escapes the charge of idiocy for very long. It is not difficult to convince anyone who has ever been to court that the problem of the incompetent judge is one of surpassing prominence. The most ironclad protection against the prejudiced or incompetent judge is a system of tightly crafted, idiot-proof rules. Where such a scheme can be designed, the discretion of the trial court is so circumscribed that little damage can be done that cannot be corrected on appeal. If, as in business, people contemplate rules before arranging their bargains, there is no objection to Rhadamanthine enforcement of simple rules that everyone should have understood in advance.

Yet the element of predictability that is achieved by means of ruthless abstraction, like the element of protection from an incompetent judge that is achieved by means of ironclad rules, can exist only where everyone understands the rules in advance and where the number of permutations of a general legal problem is comparatively small. That happy circumstance occurs in murder cases and money cases but not in domestic cases, where each suit presents a latticework of issues. Neither a single model solution nor even a set of four or five model solutions would work satisfactorily. More to the point, it makes little sense to hold people to any preconceived general rules. The likelihood is that the litigants would have been ignorant of those rules in advance and that even if they had been aware of them, they could not have followed their precepts on a day-to-day basis.

How well, then, do we achieve the desirable goals of fair general rules, predictability, and protection from judicial caprice in domestic cases? The answer is that we do not achieve either predictability or protection from caprice very well because these seemingly desirable goals require an unacceptable sacrifice of flexibility. On balance, flexibility is usually used intelligently, but this generality is little consolation to the domestic litigant who gets a completely unexpected and, by anyone's standards, capricious result from a benighted divorce court.

Throughout all of American civil law the goal of flexibility competes with the goals of predictability and protection from caprice. The goal of flexibility is not uniformly well regarded by the general public, however, because it makes judges and lawyers too terrifying. It is, therefore, considered good form by lawyers and judges to present the impression that law consists of fair general rules that are applied with ruthless consistency. What has in fact occurred, however, is that in the interest of fairness we have created a host of often conflicting general rules, from among which the judges can select the ones that render the best result in a given case. The illusion of consistency and the required flexibility are thereby both preserved. Obviously, the selection of a rule as the "best" one varies from judge to judge. The basic issue in domestic courts is how people should behave toward one another. In our complex society, the determination of so large an issue will inevitably be highly subjective.

According to anthropologists, primitive societies have little litigation. People are expected not to kill, maim, rape, or rob one another; when a crime occurs, the community convenes to apply a sanction through the village chief, village council, or even a local judge. The same simplicity exists in their civil law. They do not need the plethora of rules and counterrules that we require because life among primitives follows a simpler course.

In primitive societies there is a comparatively even distribution of wealth and a highly circumscribed set of options concerning how a person can live. These two circumstances help to generate a consensus about how personal relationships should be ordered. If there are no jobs other than homemaking for women, then there is no difference of opinion concerning how responsibilities in two-income families should be allocated. A broad social consensus allows a simple code of conduct to be a just code of conduct.

As society becomes more complex, political cleavages in the overall fabric develop that must be accommodated in the legal structure. At the heart of these political cleavages there is usually an inequality in the distribution of wealth, prestige, or opportunity. The controversy surrounding our current divorce laws is intimately connected with the nationwide debate regarding women's rights, responsibilities, and roles. At the heart of that debate is the observed disparity in wealth, prestige, and opportunity between men and women. As the consensus about appropriate behavior recedes in the face of disparities in the distribution of wealth and diversity of opinion on social issues, the law must develop new mechanisms for accommodating the lack of consensus. This process of accommodation inevitably produces complexity.

Every decade brings new economic and social problems that must be addressed by the law, but the old problems do not simultaneously disappear. For example, twenty years ago there was no need to regulate credit cards. Only businesspersons who traveled extensively or wanted a convenient record of expenses used credit cards. Society was organized on the basis of cash, individual charge accounts, and checks. Being denied a credit card was then only an annoyance. Today, however, a number of activities from registering at a hotel to renting a car require a major credit card. Mail-order houses want credit card numbers; stores want credit cards for identification before accepting checks; and the individual store charge account is rapidly disappearing. Eventually, access to credit cards will need to be regulated. Yet all the old laws concerning cash, checks, and charge accounts must remain on the books to be applied by the courts on a daily basis and, in the interim, will guide, obscure, or obstruct development of new laws.

In Chapter 1 I explored how domestic law must accommodate the interests of diverse constituencies. It must do justice for young couples without children, middle-aged couples with children, older couples with grown children, and couples in second or third marriages. Furthermore, each of these groups entered into marriage with different expectations, and each brought to marriage social conditioning from their generation, ethnic or religious group, and geographical locale. The problems that need to be addressed are so diverse that applying broad principles like the ones that control domestic matters in primitive societies would accomplish nothing. What is needed is a set of discrete, narrow principles tailored to specific categories of cases.

Indeed, domestic law is characterized by such principles. There are, in fact, numerous principles, many of them conflicting, so that lawyers are often unable to determine in advance which principles the trial court judge will apply to any given case. Not only do we have on the statute books or in the court-made decisional law new divorce principles like no-fault, designed for young, mobile, and independent people; in addition, we still have most of the rules that were developed fifty or more years ago when America disapproved of divorce and acted as primitive societies do. All these highly contradictory rules can be trotted out on appropriate occasions. They can also be trotted out on inappropriate occasions. The middle-aged housewife who expects to be treated according to the terms under which she married and is faced with an uninformed judge who applies the new principles of no-fault designed for childless couples in their twenties is utterly thunderstruck.

The mechanics of this terrifying "rule selection process" might spring to life if we take a hypothetical but realistic example. For as long as anyone can remember, abandonment by one spouse of the other has been grounds for a fault-based divorce. Let us assume that John and Mary have been married for fifteen years and that one day John packs his bags, leaves Mary, rents a new apartment, and takes a new job in a city five hundred miles away. Has John "abandoned" Mary? He may or may not have, depending on the surrounding facts and, more important, depending on how the judge abstracts the facts in his or her own mind to fit them into the preconceived legal category of "abandonment."

If Mary has been the traditional "dutiful" wife who has always been willing to move wherever John wanted to live, and if John just decided that he wanted to be alone or live with another woman, then John has clearly abandoned Mary. But what if John is a business executive with the Ajax Corporation and Ajax has transferred him from a pleasant city to rural Backwater where Mary does not want to live? Under the traditional rules of domestic law John, being the husband, is considered the primary breadwinner in the family, and Mary is obligated to move wherever his economic prospects are brightest. Under the old rules, if Mary has refused to move to Backwater, she has abandoned John.

The law of abandonment that gave the husband the un-qualified right to select the marriage domicile made sense when the employment opportunities for women were lim-ited. Today, however, the law is unworkable when applied to many two-income households. How, for example, do we apply the law if Mary is a big-city lawyer who makes $10,000 a year more than John? Does *she* then become the primary breadwinner, and must John organize his life around her career even if it means leaving Ajax and becom-ing a bus driver? Certainly not, but at the same time John will have an uphill fight convincing a court that Mary is "at fault" because she will not go to Backwater where her sophisticated legal skills are largely useless. If Mary is happy to stay married and see John on weekends but John wants a full-time wife and files for divorce, he will probably be treated less favorably than he would be if Mary were the party insisting on the divorce. On the other hand, if both parties want a divorce, the court would probably not allow either party to claim abandonment and would process the case on a no-fault basis.

Typically, when both husband and wife work, the hus-band enjoys a distinctly higher salary. Statistically, when the wife works full time, her income is less than 35 percent of the family income. Mary, then, is probably not a lawyer. Suppose that she is a housewife who works part time in a local museum making about $8,000 a year. John makes $50,000 a year, but Mary is unwilling to leave the city and its cultural life for the smokestacks and cultural deprivation of Backwater. John is still the primary breadwinner. Should a court order him to pay alimony if Mary won't move? Nobody knows for sure.

John may not want a divorce, but he also may not want to support a separate household exclusively for Mary's use.

Furthermore, John may think that he is entitled to Mary's company and emotional support in return for his financial support, but Mary would rather be dead than live in Backwater. The question of whether a divorce should be granted on the fault-based theory of abandonment or under no-fault becomes crucial to the resolution of a number of issues, such as alimony and, depending on the state, child custody and property division.

Yet the determination of whether to handle the divorce on fault or no-fault principles is highly subjective to the judge. If John can get the divorce processed on fault grounds by successfully arguing abandonment because Mary refused to move with him when his job required a transfer, then Mary gets no alimony. On the other hand, if Mary can convince the court that no blame attaches to her refusal to move and force the case to proceed under no-fault, she can get alimony because of the economic need associated with her employment opportunities, which are limited even in a large urban area. In many jurisdictions the distribution of marital property, including property titled in John's name alone, would also depend on whether there was a finding of fault at the time of the divorce. If Mary can convince the court that John was at fault, she might enhance her alimony award, because traditionally alimony has also been used as a penalty.

Once John has moved to Backwater and the couple have been separated for a year without making any progress toward solving their geography problem, they can either bang out a settlement themselves with the help of their lawyers or go to court and play judicial roulette. If they choose the latter course, the game will probably proceed somewhat as follows: If Mary initiates the action on a no-fault ground, such as one year's voluntary separation, John may countersue on the fault-based grounds of abandonment. At that point, it will become obvious to Mary's lawyer that John's allegation of fault should be met with a fault-based counterclaim on Mary's part, which will probably be a charge of mental cruelty. Mary will allege that John humiliated her, was indifferent to her sexual and emotional needs, and put his work ahead of his family when it was not necessary to his career. In this way Mary's lawyer will attempt to argue that divorce was inevitable before John's move to Backwater and that Mary has always had fault-based grounds. John's lawyer, who is no slouch, will then amend John's original divorce complaint to allege mental cruelty on the part of Mary.

Now, if John and Mary have been separated for a year or so, it is not unlikely that both John and Mary will have wanted companionship of the opposite sex. If either one has been indiscreet, the other can also claim adultery, which in domestic court has traditionally been a showstopper. Let us complicate the scenario, then, much as it is often complicated in real life, by assuming that John has indiscreetly acquired a live-in housemate of the opposite sex.

As recently as twenty years ago there was an informal hierarchy of fault-based grounds for divorce. Ordinarily, adultery dwarfed all other grounds for divorce, and abandonment was usually considered more serious than the nebulous ground of mental cruelty, particularly since mental cruelty was actually the earliest concession to our need for letting people out of hopelessly bad matches. Today, however, the rules are unclear concerning whether adultery outweighs mental cruelty, whether abandonment outweighs adultery, or whether cruelty offsets cruelty. Because sex in general is no longer considered by a majority the exclusive province of married couples, it is not surprising that adultery has lost its position as the ultimate weapon on the domestic battlefield. However, courts usually distinguish between adultery that causes the breakup of a marriage and adultery that takes place after an irretrievable rupture has occurred but before a divorce is awarded.

Moreover, if John and Mary have young children at home, a whole new set of problems arises. Who is better able to care for the children—John, with his $50,000 income living in a nice house in Backwater? Or Mary, who must now scratch for a full-time job and live in a small apartment? With whom do the children want to live and for what reasons? If the judge believes that Mary is at fault and that John is blameless, he or she may decide the question of the "best interests of the children" in John's favor, and the judge can justify the conclusion by pointing to John's income; his new large house; and the law-abiding, peaceful nature of Backwater. Deciding the custody issue this way would be a classic example of how judges arrive at decisions based on their total perception of real-life fairness but then articulate their results in the "slave language" of preconceived legal categories that is demanded by appellate courts. The legal requirement is to award custody to the parent who will better care for the children; the judge, however, can characterize John's and Mary's respective child-rearing abilities in any way that achieves what he or she thinks is a fair overall result.

But the judge probably would not give the children to John. The judge can conclude that although Mary is at fault she has the stronger relationship with the children and will be a better single parent. John, then, would need to pay about $1,500 a month child support—but no alimony, since no-fault—so Mary could afford to live in a decent place (or Mary could be awarded the use of the family house on which John must still pay the mortgage). In this way Mary can continue the work she enjoys at the museum while being able to spend a lot of time with the children—hardly a great result from John's point of view.

Furthermore, notwithstanding all the complaints and countercomplaints, the trial court judge can elect to decide the case on a no-fault basis. Where both parties are at fault, no divorce can be allowed on a fault ground to either party. But all fault is relative. If the judge decides that Mary's abandonment justified John's adultery, then both sides are at fault. If, however, the judge considers that Mary might eventually have made it up with John except for his grievous fault in committing adultery, then Mary wins on the fault theory. And the judge could consider Mary's abandonment so serious as to have justified John's adultery and grant the divorce to John on the basis of Mary's fault. All these decisions are perfectly consistent with some existing principle in domestic law. An appellate court could reverse any of them by deciding to apply a principle different from the one applied by the trial court, but such a decision would not necessarily be any more correct, or even any more predictable, than the original decision given by the trial court judge. The appellate court, of course, would be correct in the legal sense because it is more powerful and its decision is final.

The moral of the tale of John and Mary is that, within certain broad bounds, the trial court judge can select from a smorgasbord of rules and counterrules to arrive at any conclusion that he or she thinks is fair. Nonetheless, the existence of preconceived legal rules makes it necessary in every case to abstract all the elements of a personal relationship so that they fit appropriate legal categories. Because this process of abstraction is an artificial one, it often leads to absurd results. Court decisions are dependent, at least in part, on the skill of the parties' respective lawyers in playing the abstraction game.

At the heart of John and Mary's problem are two people who are divorcing because each is uncompromising. John is unwilling to quit Ajax, take a cut in salary, and find another job to save his marriage. Mary is unwilling to submerge her cultural needs long enough for John to complete his tour of duty in Backwater. Neither has really abandoned the other, and neither has been particularly cruel. The adultery issue is a red herring, since it did not cause the breakup. What is really at issue is how to handle the relative poverty Mary and the children will experience when the economies of a joint household are lost. The children are the ones who will suffer most acutely. Inevitably, they will lose either their mother or their father. If they are young, custody will probably be awarded to Mary, and a court can only slightly mitigate the children's newfound poverty by forcing John to provide for them. John resents this; he does not want to pay for children he does not see. And, of course, a court can do nothing about the emotional trauma that the loss of a parent entails for children or that the loss of children entails for a parent.

If John and Mary perceived their problem in the way I have just explained it (and I have to be right because I created the characters), then they would compromise and not get divorced. But the whole thing is subjective. In

John's mind, Mary is wrong not to help him with his career; in Mary's mind, John is selfish and thinks only of himself. From that position it is an easy step to urge abandonment, cruelty, and ultimately adultery against each other. Some judges would sort out the problem exactly as I have; others would be impressed by abandonment, cruelty, or adultery arguments. The judge who favors men would accept abandonment; the judge who favors women would accept cruelty; and the moralistic judge would be impressed by adultery. To make matters worse, the appellate judges will have their turn at abstracting the facts and fitting them into what they consider to be the appropriate legal categories.

In fact, none of the preconceived legal categories relating to fault-based divorces is particularly applicable to the case of John and Mary. John and Mary are not really fighting about John's cruelty to Mary or Mary's abandonment of John; they are merely the victims of a growing lack of congruence in what each expects from life. Furthermore, they are both victims of today's cultural conditioning, which encourages rather than discourages divorce. Once society allows the conclusion that divorce is as good a situation as staying married, many of yesteryear's incentives to compromise vanish. Conceivably, both John and Mary would like to stay married—but only on his or her own terms. Since neither will acquiesce in the other's terms, divorce becomes inevitable. The intelligent questions to be asked, then, do not concern the preconceived legal categories of fault but rather how a separation can be structured that will best accommodate both parties so that the least violence will be done to each and to the children. Ironically, it often happens that the solution salvaging the most from a bad mess is beyond a court's power to impose.

If the parties themselves are conciliatory, and, more important, if their lawyers encourage fair compromise, it may occur to everyone that both John and Mary will achieve more of what each wants through a negotiation process that eliminates translations and addresses exactly what concerns each person. For example, Mary may be resentful that she cannot earn more than $8,000 a year doing unskilled work. John, on the other hand, may be disinclined to support Mary through the rest of her life merely because she is middle-aged and has dim current prospects for future employment. Ideally, then, John might agree to borrow $50,000 in one lump sum—something a court has no power to order—so that Mary can finish college and go to graduate school. It might then be agreed that Mary will support the children as well as herself from the $50,000 for as long as it takes for the children to finish high school and for her to complete her education.

In this way John has once and for all discharged his obligation to Mary and the children, and he can start his life over. Although Mary cannot contract away John's obligation to support the children, any liability John might have toward the children if Mary should dissipate the money prematurely can be prevented by putting the $50,000 in trust and directing the trustee as to how the money is to be disbursed. Mary gets the children when they are in school; John has them during the summer. John can, and probably will, want to help with the children's college education, but that is not an immediate legal problem—it can be solved by a three-way partnership among John, Mary, and the children.

Although a lump-sum settlement is not the arrangement that everyone would want, it might well best satisfy John and Mary. Mary may be pleased that she has the money in hand and need not worry about the regularity of future payments, and John knows the limits of his liability. Once he has paid off the loan to make the settlement, his finances are his own. Mary probably gets a little less than she would get from court-ordered alimony, but a bank then bears the risk that John will lose his job, die, remarry, or just default.

In almost every American jurisdiction a divorce court is empowered to distribute a couple's property. In the eight community-property states of the West, of which California is the most prominent, a fifty-fifty split of all assets acquired during the marriage is the norm. In the common-law states of the East and the Middle West courts have varying powers to give property belonging to one spouse to the other. Many states exclude from the pool of property everything acquired by one spouse before the marriage as well as everything received by either spouse through gift or inheritance. All assets acquired through joint efforts, however (and it is usually considered that a woman's work as a wife and homemaker constitutes recognizable effort toward the acquisition of property), are equitably split at the time of divorce. Thus, the fact that all property is in the husband's name does not prevent, at least in theory, the wife from getting her fair share.

Approximately half the non-community-property states that permit equitable distribution allow decisions about property to be influenced by considerations of fault, the economic circumstances of the parties, and what the parties plan to do after divorce. The other non-community-property states limit their inquiry to a determination of how much wealth was acquired during the marriage and the fair contribution of each spouse to that wealth.

The determination of questions such as these brings a whole new dimension to the expression "can of worms." What happens if during the course of a marriage a man lives frugally—buying few clothes, driving an old car, traveling little, and supporting no hobbies—while his wife spends money as if it were going out of style? Is the bulk of the money saved through the marriage the result of the husband's forbearance and therefore his, or does the wife share equally? What if the husband has satisfied his needs lavishly while keeping his wife on a strict allowance? Has the accumulation of a surplus during the marriage been the result of the wife's sacrifice? Delicate analytical questions like these are often eliminated in the common-law states by the presumption of equal division that prevails in the community-property states.

Even where the rules are simple, questions about property can be kept within manageable bounds only when the assets are tangible and divisible; for example, houses, bank accounts, stocks, and bonds. When, however, there is an interest in a business where the owners are active managers, or an interest in nonvested pensions, even simple rules about division cannot be applied because splitting the assets involves destroying them. If, for example, the husband owns a small firm, the company may give him a total return of $40,000 a year; however, the lion's share of that return is to his own daily work and accumulated goodwill, not to any tangible assets that can be sold on the open market.

This chapter's examples have all concerned upper-middle-class couples. That is because most divorce law is shaped by parties with enough money at stake to hire lawyers and litigate through the states' highest courts. Sadly, however, most divorcing couples have almost no property of any consequence.[1] In fact, most couples can be considered lucky if both husband and wife have job opportunities after they divorce. Most upper-middle-class Americans are mortgaged to the hilt, at least until their children are finished with school and out on their own. Rarely does a couple under thirty-five have any significant equity in a house, and the urban apartment dweller doesn't have even that.

Divorcing couples usually misunderstand the economic consequences of court-ordered remedies such as the sale of a business that has little market value or the distribution of pension credits accrued under systems like public employee plans in which the benefit is a combination of insurance and deferred compensation. Couples frequently go to court expecting the judge to accomplish the miracle of expanding the total wealth available for distribution. The judge cannot, of course, accomplish this miracle, and if a case is hotly contested, much of what property there is will go to pay lawyers and court costs.

Settlement will almost always achieve a better economic result than litigation. For example, going businesses should not be destroyed, and pensions should be left in place so that they can be harvested in old age for everyone's benefit. Unless middle-aged people are desperate to

1. This is not to say, of course, that people with little property do not fight over what few assets they do own. Hot and heavy courtroom dramas proceed every day about who gets the Victrola, the 1974 Volkswagen, or the television set and the furniture.

remarry, divorce may often be self-defeating because of loss or diminution of pension rights and Social Security. For older people formal separation is preferable.

Among upper-middle-class people I always tend to favor a "lump-sum settlement" similar to the one I proposed for John and Mary. I believe that women are better off if they have cash in the bank and that men are better off if they can put their first families behind them, at least financially, and start fresh. Women are better off because they have neither alimony collection problems nor concern about former husbands' dying, with the consequent termination of support. Furthermore, a woman can keep her cash settlement even if she remarries—something that she cannot do with alimony—and that may make a second marriage more attractive. Men are better off because after they repay whatever has been borrowed to make the lump-sum settlement they are free to do whatever they wish with their income without litigation over alimony.

The conclusion to be gleaned from this chapter, which will be reiterated later on in other contexts, is that the most dangerous approach to getting a divorce is a litigation-oriented one. Obviously, there are occasions when the parties are quarreling so violently that the first step must be a court order separating them and arranging temporary custody of children and temporary support. Thereafter, however, calm deliberation with lawyers and a careful evaluation of what each person hopes to salvage from the marriage is the course most likely to lead to conservation of limited assets and economy of legal expenses.

For those whose emotional relationships have left deep wounds, this is difficult advice to take. Sometimes the emotional rewards of litigation—of an all-or-nothing call by a neutral umpire—outweigh the economic benefits of negotiated settlements. But there is inevitably a choice: the behavior that maximizes emotional satisfaction almost inevitably will not maximize economic return. As I suggest in the next chapter, litigation that has emotional rewards for husbands and wives may have devastating effects on children.

3

Child Custody

THE economic issues already discussed are complex and their resolutions unacceptably imprecise, but they are paradigms of simplicity compared with the most emotional and explosive of all domestic issues—child custody. Fathers who do not get custody attack the system because it allegedly discriminates by sex against them; mothers who do not get custody allege a "double standard" that penalizes women for sexual behavior that is tolerated in men. Although all lawsuits produce unsuccessful, dissatisfied litigants, child custody decisions are especially prone to being turned into ideological *causes célèbres* by losers.

In the nineteenth century and the early part of this century the law tended to give fathers custody, particularly when mothers were at fault in breaking up the marriage. That rule was a logical extension of the inferior legal status of women, the husband's property right in his family's labor, and the husband's absolute obligation to support his children. But even a hundred years ago this rule made little sense in terms of human emotions; consequently, it was abolished in this century. By 1950 it was almost always the rule that a mother was the natural custodian of young children if she was a fit parent.

But the behavior that different courts characterized as evidencing "fitness" differed as dramatically as the size of judges' feet. In application, the rule of maternal preference allowed judges substantial leeway to take a mother's fault into consideration in the award of custody. It was frequently the case, therefore, that sexual "promiscuity" on the part of a woman would cause a court to declare her "unfit."

Today the presumption in favor of the mother is rapidly eroding because it discriminates against fathers on the basis of sex. Although approximately thirty-two jurisdictions retain some type of maternal preference in awarding custody of very young children, this preference has become largely a tie breaker. The emerging rule is that all custody disputes should be decided on their individual merits; the parent whom the judge considers the most competent should receive custody.[1] On the face of it, this emerging new rule makes eminently good sense because some fathers are surpassingly desirable parents and some mothers are child abusers. Unfortunately, the new sex-neutral approach is not an advance in domestic relations law because of the inherently distorting effect of going to court. This chapter

1. It is impossible to summarize the exact nature of the law throughout the fifty states and the District of Columbia on this subject because courts and legislatures are changing it from day to day. To make matters worse, although most jurisdictions use similar terminology (e.g., "maternal presumption," "tender years doctrine"), the meanings that they attach to this legal jargon often differ. In general, the states can be divided into three classes: (1) those with no maternal presumption; (2) those with a weak maternal presumption; and (3) those with a strong maternal presumption. The states with the strong maternal presumption require a fairly high order of proof of a father's superior parental ability before awarding him custody; those with a weak maternal presumption use the presumption only as a tie breaker. All states that indulge in a maternal presumption appear to permit the presumption to be rebutted if it can be shown that the award of custody to the father will be in the "best interests of the child."

is about how the process of sorting out custody problems in court affects those problems, usually for the worse.

When I was first practicing law, I avoided starvation by handling divorce cases. In rural areas a lawyer either tries divorce cases or searches land titles; since I find real estate practice consummately dull, I opted for divorce cases to pay my rent. Although I represented men and women about equally in the three years that I applied myself to the divorce court trade, I never represented a father who wanted custody of his children. I do not infer from this experience a total absence of men willing to risk death to keep their children, but I do infer that such men are rare. Through the years I have consulted practicing lawyers around the country on this subject, and they confirm my experience. It is an extraordinary man who wants to take care of a two-year-old from morning till night. In my experience, fathers who are awarded custody of young children delegate actual child care to a female, often their own mothers.

My faith in mothers as more dedicated parents is not just outdated and uninformed homespun wisdom. In 1977 Sharon Araji of Washington State University published a study entitled "Husbands' and Wives' Attitude-Behavior Congruence on Family Roles." In plain English, she asked

In 1978 there were twenty jurisdictions that allowed no presumption: Alaska, Arizona, California, Colorado, Connecticut, Delaware, District of Columbia, Georgia, Hawaii, Illinois, Indiana, Iowa, Maine, Massachusetts, Michigan, Nebraska, North Carolina, Ohio, Texas, and Washington. The states with a strong (but still rebuttable) presumption included Mississippi, New Hampshire, New Jersey, Rhode Island, Tennessee, and Utah. The remaining twenty-five states seemed to use the maternal presumption only for young children if all other things were equal. Arkansas, for example, appeared to have a maternal presumption only for young children of the female sex. (West Virginia is a special case and will be discussed later on in the text.) See Sanford Katz and Monroe Inker, *Fathers, Husbands and Lovers* (American Bar Association Press, 1979), pp. 161–81.

her subjects what they believed the proper division of family labor should be and then asked how, in fact, such work was divided. More than two-thirds of those asked how child care *should* be divided responded that the division should be equal. When asked about actual performance, however, those same individuals overwhelmingly responded that it was the woman who bore the brunt of child care duties. Sharing responsibility for child care would seem to be more a cosmopolitan pretension than a common practice.

Another study, done at the University of Nevada that same year—"The Division of Labor Among Cohabiting and Married Couples," by Rebecca Stafford, Elaine Bachman, and Pamela Dibona—found that division of labor within the household remained resistant to change. Furthermore, responsibility for the maintenance of children was among the duties least often shared. To the extent that husbands participated in child care at all, they were more likely to be involved in playing, baby-sitting, and disciplining rather than in such day-to-day tasks as feeding, changing, and bathing. The Nevada study is significant also because it examined cohabiting couples as well as married ones. One might think that those cohabiting would exhibit more progressive attitudes toward division of domestic responsibilities, but the study found that such couples exhibited a remarkable adherence to the sexual stereotypes of the world in which they grew up.

Finally, "Problems of Professional Couples" by Norma Heckman, Rebecca Bryson, and Jeff Bryson, a study of professional couples done at San Diego State University, found that even among highly career-oriented women it was taken as a given by both spouses that the woman had the primary child care responsibilities. The role of mother was seen as far more limiting than that of wife. One of the study's crucial findings was that the decision to take primary responsibility for children was frequently a voluntary one for women who saw parenting as a fundamental part of a successful female life.

The fact that women as a group are either more enthusiastic about parenting or simply do more of it because that is how labor is divided in their homes does not mean, of course, that in every case the mother is the better parent. Fathers who want to retain the companionship of their children and who believe that under single-parent conditions they would be better parents than their wives expect the judicial system to operate on more refined principles than simple statistical discrimination.

Fathers are now demanding that courts award custody based on an individualized inquiry into the specific parent-child relationships in their particular families. All this appears reasonable until we understand just how much sinister bargaining is carried on in the shadow of this unpredictable, individual-oriented system.

The individual approach, in fact, would be unexceptionable if courts actually considered the relative merits of the parents in each case. Very few divorce cases, however, ever get to court. Nationwide, about 92 percent of all divorces are settled without a courtroom encounter. Divorce decrees are typically drafted by the lawyers for the parties after private compromise, and these compromises are then approved by a judge. Mothers routinely sacrifice necessary financial support in order to get custody of their children without a fight. This distasteful form of barter is one of the reasons that single women with dependent children are becoming a new class of the poverty-stricken.

My first experience with the use of the divorce laws' unpredictability to terrorize women into trading away their support occurred soon after I began my career as a small-town lawyer. My client was a railroad brakeman who had fallen out of love with his wife and in love with motorcycles. Along the way he had met a woman who was as taken with motorcycles as he. After about a year my client's wife filed for divorce. My client had two children at home—one about nine and the other about twelve. Unfortunately for him, the judge in the county where his wife had filed her suit was notorious for giving high alimony and child support awards. The last thing that I wanted to do was go to trial. The wife had a strong case of adultery against my client, and the best my client could come up with as a defense was a lame countersuit for "cruel and inhuman treatment"— not a showstopper in a rural domestic court fourteen years ago.

During the initial interview I asked my client about his children, and he told me that he got along well with them. When I asked whether he wanted custody, he emphatically indicated that two children were the last thing he wanted from divorce. Nonetheless, it occurred to me that if my client developed a passionate attachment to his children and told his wife that he would fight for custody all the way to the state supreme court, we might settle the whole divorce fairly cheaply. My client was a quick study; that night he went home and began a campaign focusing on the children. His likelihood of getting custody from the judge was virtually nonexistent, but that did not discourage our blustering threats.

My client's wife, as I had hoped, was unwilling to take any chance, no matter how slight, on losing her children. Consequently, the divorce was settled exactly as I wanted.

The wife got the children by agreement, along with very modest alimony and child support. All we had needed to defeat her legitimate claims in the settlement process was a halfway credible threat of a protracted custody battle. As Solomon showed us, the better a mother is as a parent, the less likely she is to allow a destructive fight over her children.

We are led to an inescapable conclusion: a sex-neutral approach has the unintended effect of terrorizing mothers into accepting bad deals. In the end, on statistical average, women come out of divorce settlements under our purportedly sex-neutral system with the worst of all worlds: they get the children but insufficient or no money with which to support them.

An important reason that little attention has been given to the effect of in-court rules on out-of-court bargaining is that our views on divorce are informed more by wishful thinking than by the facts of life. Many men begin with a political conviction that women *ought* to be equal to men economically, and then we make the insupportable leap to the conclusion that women *are* equal to men economically. It then logically follows that women can support children as well as men and that whoever wants the children can pay for them.

In the real world, however, women are much poorer than men, and this pattern is highly resistant to change. This proposition is supported by the fact that 34.1 percent of all previously married female heads of households receive public assistance, although only 1.8 percent of households headed by a husband and wife receive such assistance.[2] The cost of child care itself in terms of lost working time is a major part of the economic burden placed

2. This figure does not include never-married female heads of households, 64 percent of whom receive public assistance.

on single mothers. For example, previously married females without children average 35.6 weeks of work a year, whereas previously married females with children average only 28.3 weeks of work a year. Once children are old enough to care for themselves, the economic performance of households headed by previously married females improves significantly. Only 14 percent of all child welfare payments go to families in which all children are over twelve.

Ideally, in a domestic case we want to take a broken-down marriage and sort out emotional and economic problems. The children should go with the parent who will care for them best, with due regard to how strong their bond is with that parent; to his or her ability to provide financially; and to his or her capacity for love, concern, leadership, and emotional support. Similarly, we want to allocate economic benefits—either alimony or property division—to reflect relative degrees of fault in the breakup of the marriage as well as the economic needs of the parties. Central to this latter consideration is whether one party has responsibility for supporting the children.

Although divorce requires a court order, most court orders are entered at the behest of both parties who have agreed to a settlement. The judge merely signs the agreed-to order presented by counsel. On a typical morning a domestic judge will sign as many as thirty divorce decrees. The busier the court and the more harried the judge, the less attention he or she gives to the equity of the settlements. Judges, it must be stressed, do not enjoy extra work any more than do posthole diggers or elevator operators. If a bargain is good enough for the litigants and their lawyers, it is usually good enough for the judge. The judge supposedly supervises the fairness of these settlements, but this rarely occurs in busy courts unless the agreement is so outrageously one-sided that its inequity almost leaps off the page.

The everyday occurrence of children being traded for money should be sufficient in and of itself to invite a re-evaluation of a system that puts custody awards up for grabs. Yet there are additional reasons for questioning the wisdom of our apparently fair, sex-neutral system that relate directly to the welfare of children. Those who have studied family relations, such as the famous lawyer/psychoanalyst team of Joseph Goldstein, Anna Freud, and Albert Solnit, after extensive study of children under the strain of divorce, found that custody decisions should be made quickly. Protracted hassles over custody undermine a child's sense of security, and once a child is placed in one environment he or she should not be moved to another. Their research indicates that from the point of view of the child's best interests—supposedly the legal standard—differences in relative parenting ability are less important than both the speed and permanency of custody arrangements. The current system for handling child-related matters, involving as it does years of possible litigation, is calculated to produce results that thoughtful scientists consider contrary to the child's best interests.

All courts are in the business of measuring things. But in domestic litigation the measurements are qualitatively different from other measurements that courts routinely make. Courts are designed to deal with discrete issues and tangible evidence. Did Hatfield shoot McCoy? Did PepsiCo steal Coca-Cola's trade secret? Domestic courts are asked to be moral arbiters of the righteousness of lives. The problem is not that courts are incompetent to make such decisions but rather that the sheer complexity of their task means that the measurement process itself changes the thing that is measured.

Lack of neutrality in measuring things is a recurring problem in many areas of human endeavor. In physics the problem is known as the Heisenberg uncertainty principle —which refers to Werner Heisenberg's discovery that it is impossible to measure both the speed and the location of an electron simultaneously because the measuring devices themselves affect the speed and location being measured. A similar principle applies to divorce cases, and measuring family problems usually makes those problems worse.

THE way divorces are handled in practice by underpaid lawyers and overworked courts gives rise to a fundamental proposition: all divorce law must be crafted with a view to voluntary settlements and not to courtroom litigation. A rule that is wondrously fair when it is actually used before a judge can have a distortive effect in out-of-court settlements. In order to make this proposition spring to life, let us take the hypothetical case of Steve and Jane who are about to get divorced in a state like Iowa, where in contested cases children are awarded to the better parent, after exhaustive judicial inquiry into the parenting ability of each.

Steve and Jane are a typical middle-class couple. Steve graduated from a good midwestern university, and Jane married him after completing her second year of college. They have two children, a boy aged seven and a girl aged four. Steve is a salesman with a large company and makes about $27,000 a year; Jane works part time as a buyer in a department store and earns about $10,000 a year. Steve sells office equipment. His territory is his own city, so he is not required to travel or work at night. Steve is a good parent; he spends several hours with the children each evening. On the weekends Steve makes every effort to include the children in chores, like painting, that he does around the house, and he tries to take them on at least one outing a week to a sporting event, the zoo, a park, or the local swimming pool.

Jane, on the other hand, has been the primary caretaker of the children. When their son was born, Jane left work to stay home with the baby, and she did not return to work until their daughter was in nursery school. She arranges her part-time work around the children's schedule so that she is home when they are home, and one of the conditions of her job is that she can stay home if her children are sick. Jane often gets frustrated by the children; she does a lot of yelling and occasionally spanks them without justification, but on balance she is a good parent. She reads with her children, teaches them arithmetic, discourages them from watching television excessively, and spends her time at home in active parenting.

Steve, on his side, is a good provider. Although Steve and Jane bicker in the usual way about money, they agree that the children come first. Neither Steve nor Jane has done anything reprehensible in the marriage; they have just come to thoroughly bore each other. They have nothing in common except for the children and they fantasize that if divorced each could find a more sympathetic, supportive, and amusing mate. Their decision to divorce is mutual, and they contemplate a no-fault proceeding. Jane, who has the closer relationship with the children because she spends more time with them, wants the children and would not give them up under any circumstances. Steve understands that he is unsuited to care for young children day in and day out, and he also understands that his social life after divorce will be circumscribed if he has children to tie him down.

Ideally, Steve and Jane would agree that Jane will keep the children. Steve will have unlimited visitation rights, and the children will stay with him whenever he wants—weekends, summer vacations, and holidays.[3] Since Jane is young and can both earn a salary and remarry, it is not expected that Steve will pay alimony, but he will pay about $500 a month child support so that the children can continue to enjoy their current standard of living. Jane will work more hours to increase her income to $15,000 a year, and some type of day-care arrangement will be made to take care of the children while she is at work.

I have drawn a portrait of an entirely reasonable couple who understand the advantages and disadvantages of divorce. Most important, they have taken into consideration the children's needs and have organized their settlement with the welfare of the children at least partially in mind. Steve and Jane have done their best to accommodate everyone's interest, and if they continue to be reasonable and conciliatory, the judicial process will not distort their divorce arrangements.

If, however, we change the scenario a little, as it would

3. This is conceivably a case where "joint custody" might work well if it is understood that Jane will continue to provide the children's principal residence with all that implies in the way of schools, churches, and ties to the community. The advantage of joint custody is that Steve can then give permission for such things as school outings and lifesaving medical procedures, and he can otherwise dispatch administrative details of the children's lives when Jane is unavailable. Joint custody, however, is a remedy that requires a high degree of cooperation between the parents. It is discussed at length later on in this chapter.

probably be changed in real life, the Heisenberg uncertainty principle immediately enters the picture. Suppose that Steve is not a bad fellow, but he is convinced that his marriage is breaking up largely because of Jane's unreasonable demands. Jane likes to "keep up with the Joneses" and demands money for competitive social purposes—membership in a country club, entertaining, new clothes, and the like. Steve, on the other hand, is indifferent to his position in the social pecking order; he likes to attend sporting events, play on neighborhood teams, watch television, and tinker around the house. Most of his marital troubles stem from his inability to satisfy his wife's consumption demands on his modest salary. Because he cannot increase his income, he feels inadequate.

Jane, who is still attractive and vivacious, believes that Steve is a social bore. She perceives her own interests, not as social climbing, but as an effort to give a cultural dimension to her family's life. She does not find sitting in a ball park stimulating, and she is convinced that the daily ration of television in her home is turning her and her children into vegetables. In this instance the decision to divorce is still mutual, but it is made before the negotiations about financial terms are complete.

When it finally dawns on Steve that he will need to pay Jane and the children $500 a month *after taxes,* roughly one-third of his take-home pay, he becomes resentful. Steve consults a lawyer and some hard bargaining begins. The lawyer will not be philosophical about Jane's needs; the job of any lawyer is to get the best deal he or she can for the client. If a lawyer takes into consideration the problems of the adverse party, the lawyer has essentially sold out his or her client.

From a tactical point of view, Steve's biggest weapon is a *potential* fight over custody. As mentioned earlier, Jane would not countenance a divorce if she thought it might entail loss of the children. If Steve starts talking about how he wants the children with him, or at least wants "joint custody," Jane must reconsider her position on divorce and her financial demands. Inevitably, Jane too will hire a lawyer.

Jane's lawyer will tell her that in all likelihood a court will award her the children; however, the lawyer will qualify that prediction by pointing out that it is always possible to get a woman-hating judge who will award Steve custody or will award joint custody. What are the chances of losing custody? The lawyer concludes there is about a 5 percent chance that Steve would get the children and about a 25 percent chance of some type of joint custody. Horrified, Jane asks why. The lawyer replies that judges are unpredictable—a perfectly accurate answer.

It should be remembered that at this stage nobody has filed divorce papers in court. Yet the prospect of divorce— with everyone taking the advice of lawyers who are trying to set their clients up for a courtroom drama—has set the Heisenberg uncertainty principle in motion as both parties alter their behavior with an eye toward the upcoming litigation. Steve may work feverishly to establish a pattern of child care that will make him eligible for custody; Jane may try to create some ground for a fault-based divorce, thus raising the specter of alimony in addition to child support.

Since the bottom line is that Steve wants to save money and Jane wants to keep the children, the compromise that immediately comes to mind is the one that I posited as the general rule: Jane gets the children and Steve contributes a small amount for their maintenance. This may appear to be reasonable until Jane realizes just how poor she will be when the joint household is dissolved. She can get a higher-paying job, but then she will work herself to a frazzle being both a mother and a primary breadwinner.

Jane, of course, can take her chances on the judicial roulette wheel. However, the better mother she is—the stronger her bonds with the children and the more intense her love for them—the less likely she is to go to court over custody. For a devoted mother to go to court over children as anything but a last resort is almost unthinkable. The odds are overwhelmingly in her favor, but *any* risk of losing is too big a risk.

If we change Steve and Jane's hypothetical circumstances slightly once again, we can see that the prospect of litigation distorts the lives of the litigants in direct proportion to the level of contention. What if Jane's dissatisfaction with her marriage has led her to have an affair? In that case, Steve has fault-based grounds for divorce, but Jane's sexual behavior does not make Steve any closer to the children, nor, for that matter, the better custodian under single-parent conditions. Nonetheless, in some jurisdictions Steve can point to Jane's "immoral conduct" as a reason to deny her the children, and in such a jurisdiction Jane's lawyer must advise her that the likelihood of her losing custody is significantly higher than his or her original estimate, although the odds are still in her favor.

When Jane is at fault, if Steve plays the part his lawyer has written for him well, Steve can almost certainly force Jane to emerge from the divorce settlement with custody but no money. In this situation the real victims are the children. The victimization of the children will be exacerbated if Steve remarries and his life is dominated by his new family. As his emotional ties to his two oldest children become weaker, so will his concern for their financial welfare.

Let us change our assumptions once again. Assume that Steve is one of those rare men who wants his children every bit as much as his wife does. Steve is in fact more interested in securing custody than in any other aspect of the divorce. He is a good father and Jane is a good mother; for Steve the problem now is to prove that he would make the better single parent. Jane, of course, must do the same thing, but in most trial courts regardless of what the statutory or common-law rule may be, she has a leg up because she is the "primary caretaker," that is, she has spent more time with the children.

Steve has several problems to overcome: (1) he has spent less total time with the children than Jane has; (2) he has yet to prove that he knows how to prepare meals, administer to health needs, and interact with the children's friends and teachers and with other parents; (3) his work schedule is more demanding than Jane's; and (4) he will inevitably delegate more parenting to others than Jane would. But Steve's ardor is not discouraged by these hurdles, and he is willing to fight. What does his lawyer do?

Even in states with a weak maternal presumption, child custody is awarded to the parent who will do the better job of child rearing. This is called the "best interests of the child" standard, and to meet it Steve's lawyer must demonstrate that Steve is the better parent. The maternal presumption is only a tie breaker, at least in theory, and it is theory that dictates the legal *process*, if not the courtroom result. Since Steve's lawyer cannot show that Steve is better than Jane at everyday parenting responsibilities, Steve's lawyer must explore the deep, dark recesses of psychological theory to prove that in the long run the children will be better off with Steve.

This undertaking inevitably leads to the hiring of "expert witnesses"—psychologists, psychiatrists, social workers, and sociologists. These experts are paid to demonstrate that the amount of time Jane spent with the children; her experience in managing their meals and arranging for their health needs; and her familiarity with their schools, teachers, and friends are insignificant in comparison to Steve's superior aptitude for parenting and the way his personality "integrates" with the personalities of the children. The experts will advance the theory that this element of personality compatibility is preeminently important in single-parent households.

I am not in favor of expert psychological testimony. My disparagement does not come from any contempt for a science that has contributed much to the quality of our lives. Rather, it comes from my experience that in a courtroom context there is a "Gresham's law of experts": the bad experts drive out the good ones. When we hire an expert witness, we want a person with the lowest possible integrity so that he or she will lie under oath. Expert witnesses are, after all, very much like lawyers: they are paid to take a set of facts from which different inferences may be drawn and to characterize those facts so that a particular conclusion follows.

There are, indeed, cases where a mother may appear competent on the surface, but perfunctory inquiry by a trained psychologist will disclose that she is a child abuser. In fact, in marriages such as Steve and Jane's, truly careful inquiry will disclose that the father is the better parent about one time in ten. Such a careful inquiry, however, is almost impossible in the real world of lawsuits because it requires experts who combine competence and integrity in a way that is seldom found. The side with the stronger case can afford to hire only competent experts with surpassing integrity; the side with the weaker case, on the other hand, wants impressive, glib experts who are devoid of integrity. When both parents are good parents, the search of each for relative superiority will result in gibberish. Unless the judge knows the experts personally, how can he or she distinguish truth-tellers from liars when their credentials are equal on paper?

I cannot imagine an issue more subject to personal bias than a decision about which parent is better. Should children be placed with an "open, empathetic" father or a "stern but value-supporting" mother? The decision may hinge on the judge's memory of his or her own parents or on his or her distrust of an expert who averts his eyes once too often. It is unlikely that the decision will be the paradigm of custom-crafted individualized justice that the system purports to deliver.

Fortunately, most judges have an intuitive grasp of the difference between good testimony and bunkum. But unfortunately, judges in states that have a "best interests of the child" standard must allow days of testimony from a parade of highly paid experts before finally rendering a decision in favor of the mother based largely on statistical discrimination. Occasionally, one side's experts will be so overwhelmingly convincing and the other's such obvious liars that the judge can quickly sort it out. But in Steve and Jane's case the testimony would be about evenly balanced.

The judge will ultimately be impressed with the fact that Jane is closer to the children. Yet the sham hearings are bad in and of themselves because the very process of preparing experts to testify in custody cases increases the hardship for all concerned.

In order for a psychiatrist or psychologist to testify in court about so-called personality integration or similar psychological phenomena, the expert must interview parents and children, conduct tests, and possibly observe the litigants in a family setting. This very exercise can undermine the mental health of the children as well as the emotional stability of the parents. When an elaborate custody battle is anticipated, the experts will create painful situations in their efforts to substantiate the testimony they have been paid to give. In much the same way that an artillery battery can "liberate the hell out of" a peaceful hamlet, experts can create emotional imbalances in the very children they are trying to "protect."

I should point out that there are three types of child custody cases, and each must be handled differently. Children under six years old are called "children of tender years"; they are the most dependent on their parents, but they usually cannot articulate an intelligent opinion about their custody. Children between six and fourteen are also dependent on their parents, but they can usually articulate a preference concerning custody arrangements and explain their reasons. By the age of fourteen a child takes on many of the qualities of an adult; in most cases, unless geography intervenes, a child over fourteen will decide for himself or herself the parent with whom he or she wants to live regardless of what a court says.

Obviously, when we are dealing with children over six, we conceivably have some real experts on the subject of how parents and children get along. Any scheme of domestic litigation that encourages children to testify in court, however, can have a substantial effect on a child's life beyond just determining the child's custody. Usually, children do not want what is best for them; they want what is pleasant for them. If children are permitted to influence decisions about custody simply by stating a preference, the parents are placed in the position of being competitive bidders in a counterfeit currency.

Two of my own court's cases come to mind. The first involved a twelve-year-old girl who fanned the fires of a protracted interstate custody battle because she wanted to date older boys and stay out late at night; the second involved a nine-year-old boy who tried to get his custody changed because he resented his mother's demand that he devote three hours a night to his schoolwork. I have observed divorce cases that have gone on for more than a year during which time both parents vied with each other to purchase the children's affections. The result was that, whichever parent finally got custody, the children were on the high road to ruination.

This analysis brings me back to my initial proposition: the litigation process itself is not neutral. The very act of going to court does more than just sort out rights and obligations that should have been frozen at the time the divorce papers were filed. If the divorce drags through the trial and appellate courts for two years, the lawsuit itself may destroy the children who, for one or another reason, are at its center. In addition, money that would have been available to ease the transition from joint household to separate households has been diverted to lawyers, court fees, and possibly expert witnesses.

The degree to which children suffer during divorce is a

widely discussed subject. The slowly grinding machinery of the courts inevitably exacerbates the emotional stresses that any divorce causes. Preeminent among the untoward effects of custody litigation per se are uncertainty, painful psychological probing (e.g. "Who do you love more, Mommy or Daddy?"), and competitive parental bribery. The magnitude of these effects is a direct function of the time it takes to conclude the proceedings.

Time means different things to adults and children. I can remember in meticulous detail the events that transpired in my life from the age of eight until I graduated from law school. The twelve years since I became a judge, however, are largely a blur. When a person is forty, a year represents one-fortieth of his or her life; when a person is five, a year represents a fifth. A divorce is traumatic just in terms of the mother's and father's separation and, possibly, new male and female companions for each entering the scene. If the children have no idea with whom they will live or under what terms or even where, their consequent insecurity undermines their ability to function. Their relations with other children suffer; their ties to the community are threatened; and often the stress they are under causes academic failure.

In the case of Steve and Jane—an accurate composite of cases I handled as a lawyer—once a custody battle is contemplated, the relationship between parents and children changes for the worse. The overriding need to prepare for court will dominate the lives of both parents, and if the opinions of the children are to be polled—either directly through court testimony or indirectly through the probing of experts—each parent is going to attempt to poison the other parent's well. Furthermore, the parent with whom the children are living during the litigation will have an advantage in any well-poisoning operation. The guerrilla warfare among parents, and collateral relatives as well, not only makes life difficult at the time of divorce; it may also undermine children's relationships with one side of their family (their natural emotional support network) for the rest of their lives. In this regard, a term frequently used in custody battles is "brainwash."

Most of the problems of child custody litigation can be avoided by not litigating the issue in the first place. It is at this point that the wisdom of the old maternal preference, or its sex-neutral alternative, the "primary caretaker parent rule," becomes evident. The primary caretaker parent rule severely limits the adverse economic and psychological effects of litigation concerning custody, and we have adopted this rule in West Virginia. Sadly, however, the sex-neutral primary caretaker parent rule is unique to West Virginia law.

In West Virginia we do not permit a maternal preference. But we do accord an explicit and almost absolute preference to the "primary caretaker parent," which is defined as the parent who: (1) prepares the meals; (2) changes the diapers and dresses and bathes the child; (3) chauffeurs the child to school, church, friends' homes, and the like; (4) provides medical attention, monitors the child's health, and is responsible for taking the child to the doctor; and (5) interacts with the child's friends, school authorities, and other parents engaged in activities that involve the child.

This list of criteria usually spells "mother," but such is

not necessarily the case. In West Virginia we have women who pursue successful lucrative careers while their husbands take care of the children, and those caretaking fathers receive the benefit of the presumption as strongly as do traditional mothers. Furthermore, where both parents share child-rearing responsibilities equally, our courts hold hearings to determine which parent would be the better single parent. This latter situation is rare, but provision for its occurrence is evidence of the actual sex neutrality of the "primary caretaker presumption."

Our rule inevitably involves some injustice to fathers. There are instances where the primary caretaker will not be the better custodian in the long run. Yet, notwithstanding its theoretical imperfections, at the most practical level the primary caretaker parent rule acknowledges that exhaustive hearings on relative degrees of parenting rarely disclose anything but gross variations in parental ability. Permitting such hearings inevitably causes Heisenberg effects in the settlement process as well as disastrous emotional trauma for all concerned if the case goes to court.

As I asserted earlier, any rule concerning custody matters will be sex-biased. An allegedly sex-neutral rule that permits exhaustive inquiry into relative degrees of parental fitness is inevitably biased in favor of men. This bias follows from the observed pattern that in consensual divorces where there is no fight over money—either because there isn't any or because there is enough to go around—women overwhelmingly receive custody through the willing acquiescence of their husbands. Experience teaches that, if there is any possibility that the *average* mother will lose her children at divorce, she will either stay married under oppressive conditions or trade away valuable rights to ensure that she will be given custody of the children.

Adjudication is an imprecise exercise. The greatest frustration in law is that there is never a choice between systems that work and systems that do not work. The choice is always between two systems, neither one of which works particularly well. When exhaustive hearings on child custody are encouraged, the hearings themselves cause one or all of the following: (1) the competitive expenditure of money to hire experts, giving apparent advantage to the wealthier party; (2) competitive bribery of children; (3) insecurity of children based on the uncertainty of the final disposition; (4) emotional wounds created by probing experts, lawyers, and courts in an effort to determine psychological compatibility; (5) disparagement of one parent by the other and brainwashing of the children in direct proportion to opportunity; and (6) an irrational settlement of economic matters out of court.

Under West Virginia's scheme, the question of which parent, if any, is the primary caretaker is proved with lay testimony by the parties themselves and by teachers, relatives, and neighbors. Which parent does the lion's share of the chores can be satisfactorily demonstrated to a court in less than an hour. Once the primary caretaker is established, the only other question is whether that parent is a "fit parent." In this regard the court is not concerned with assessing relative degrees of fitness between parents but only with whether the primary caretaker achieves a passing grade on an objective test. It is very much like a high school examination where sixty points get you a D. All that is required is the passing D; the fact that the parent who is not the primary caretaker gets a C is irrelevant.

To be a fit parent a person must: (1) feed and clothe the child appropriately; (2) adequately supervise the child and protect him or her from harm; (3) provide habitable housing; (4) avoid extreme discipline, child abuse, and other similar vices; and (5) refrain from *grossly* immoral behavior under circumstances that would affect the child. In this last regard restrained sexual behavior does not make a parent unfit. We do not attend to traditional immorality in the abstract but only to whether the child is a party to, or is influenced by, such immorality. Whether a primary caretaker parent meets these criteria can also be determined through lay testimony, and the criteria themselves are sufficiently specific that they discourage frivolous disputation.

Furthermore, we divide children into the three age-group categories I described earlier. With regard to children of tender years, our primary caretaker presumption operates absolutely if the primary caretaker is a fit parent. When, however, we come to those children who may be able to formulate an intelligent opinion about their custody, our rule becomes more flexible. When the trial court judge is unsure about the wisdom of awarding the children to the primary caretaker, he or she may ask the children for their preference and accord that preference whatever weight he or she deems appropriate. Thus, the only experts who can rebut the primary caretaker presumption are the children. The judge is not required to take the testimony of the children, however, and will usually not do so if he or she suspects bribery or other undue influence. Nonetheless, by allowing the children to be the only acceptable experts in our courts, we do provide an escape valve in the very hard cases.

Finally, once a child reaches the age of fourteen, we permit the child to name his or her guardian if both parents are fit. Often, as might be expected, this means that the parent who makes the child's life more comfortable will get custody; but there is little alternative, since children over fourteen who are living where they do not want to live will become unhappy and ungovernable anyway. In all three types of cases, the parent who receives custody is then primarily responsible for making decisions concerning the child and for providing the child's principal home. The other parent, however, is usually accorded liberal visitation rights, including the right to have the child during holidays, part of the summer, and on some weekends.

Although West Virginia's method for handling child custody may appear insensitive, we have reduced the volume of domestic litigation over children enormously. Because litigation per se is highly damaging emotionally to children, we consider this in the best interests of our state's children. More to the point, children in West Virginia cannot be used as pawns in fights that are actually about money. Under our system a mother's lawyer can tell her that if she has been the primary caretaker and is a fit parent she has *absolutely no chance* of losing custody of very young children. The result is that questions of alimony and child support are settled on their own merits.

At this point, the reader may be desperate to interject that many of these problems could be better solved by using the newest divorce court fad, joint custody. Under joint custody, divorced parents have equal time with the children and equal say in decisions about their schooling, religious training, and lifestyle. But this does not solve the problems of trades in the settlement process because many mothers find sharing custody as terrifying as complete loss of custody.

Joint custody works well when both parents live in the same neighborhood, or at least in the same city, and so long as they can cooperate on child-rearing problems. Divorcing couples often agreed to joint custody themselves in the past, long before court-ordered joint custody became a public issue. When joint custody is by agreement, the same cooperative spirit that permitted the underlying agreement will usually permit the parents to rear a child with no more antagonism than is experienced in most married households.

Voluntary joint custody, however, must be distinguished from court-ordered joint custody. A court can order that custody be shared, but it cannot order that the parents stop bickering, stop disparaging each other, or accommodate each other in child care decisions the way married parents would. And if parents do not live close to each other joint custody can place an insupportable strain on a child's social and academic life.

Furthermore, parents must constantly give permission for one thing or another. Who decides whether the child can have a driver's license at age sixteen? Who decides when the child can date, under what conditions, and with whom? When parents can agree on an orderly allocation of responsibility for deciding these issues, there is no problem. But when the parents violently disagree—and particularly if the parents disagree because they are continuing fights left over from the marriage—the child is hopelessly confused and the parents are played off one against the other.

In West Virginia we do not encourage court-ordered joint custody, although parents can agree to such an arrangement. Elsewhere, however, legislatures are being urged to make court consideration of joint custody mandatory in all contested custody cases. In states that already encourage extensive litigation over child custody, the sparing use of joint custody may not cause any more damage than does the existing system. If the geography is right and the parents are mature, there is no reason why joint custody cannot work at least as well as, and sometimes better than, custody in one parent with visitation rights in the other. Joint custody as an option cannot be rejected out of hand, but it should be understood for what it is—a good middle ground that works occasionally when all conditions are peculiarly favorable.

The nationwide debate on child custody, including the arguments for joint custody and a greater role for fathers, demonstrates just how acutely many men—often men innocent in the breakup of their marriages—feel the loss of their children. But no matter how modern we seek to become, or how liberated we wish to be from the imprisoning hand of traditional institutions, it is not possible to create custody arrangements that satisfactorily duplicate parent-child relationships in married households. Divorce must be understood for what it is: a tragedy and a disaster.

Regardless of the custody statutes that legislatures pass, or what powers are given to domestic courts, judges are never going to be architects of a brave new world of happy, single-parent households. Courts are just salvage crews. To the extent that husbands and wives engage in their own program of damage control, they can salvage more from the ruins than can courts. In child custody the parents' own damage control amounts to continued cooperation with each other on child-related problems. The goal of such cooperation is enhancement rather than destruction of the other parent's position in the mind of the child: this involves the maturity to submerge feelings of personal animosity when the child visits the other parent or when information about the child must be exchanged.

Joint custody is, after all, just a bigger and better version of traditional visitation rights with the added dubious advantage that both parents can give legal consent for the child when required. When there is a cooperative arrangement between parents by which visitation is both extensive and smoothly accomplished, calling the scheme joint custody is entirely cosmetic. The term "joint custody" merely serves to emphasize that both parents continue to have a say in the child's future. Inevitably, if both parents are cooperative, this will be the case any way under traditional visitation. Just as inevitably, if the parents are uncooperative, joint custody will only put the child in an impossible position vis-à-vis both parents and paralyze needed action. In short, in my experience all the rhetoric about joint custody amounts to a siren song that leads us from our true course. The true course is that what a court orders is insignificant in comparison to how the parents behave. Mature parents can make a bad court order work superbly; immature parents will render the best court order less than useless.

West Virginia's scheme for handling child custody and the approach that I have offered in this chapter are little consolation to divorcing couples in New York, Iowa, or any other state that fails to understand the effect of the Heisenberg uncertainty principle in domestic law. But recognition of what actually goes on in a custody battle—that it is not just a sorting out of preexisting rights but rather a destructive process in and of itself—may help rational parents avoid such battles.

4

Paying for Divorce

ABOUT a week before Christmas in 1969 a woman—I'll call her Susan—came to my one-man law office in Fairmont. Several years before, Susan's husband had divorced her, leaving her with two children to rear. Susan's former husband was a long-haul truck driver, and after the divorce he moved from West Virginia to Ohio. Susan had been awarded $250 a month child support but had received hardly a cent in the past three years. Susan supported herself, her ten-year-old daughter, and her four-year-old son by working on the assembly line at a local factory. Her take-home pay was about $650 a month, barely enough to buy food, pay the rent, and keep her car running.

Susan had found her way to my office on a snowy December day because her husband had returned to West Virginia for a Christmas visit with his relatives. When Susan learned of his presence, she went to a local justice of the peace and swore out a nonsupport warrant, since failure to pay support is a misdemeanor criminal offense. The local sheriff arrested the husband—I'll call him Bob—and placed him in the Marion County jail. Susan then wanted me to squeeze the maximum blood from Bob before he again fled to the anonymity of Ohio's cities. At the time Bob owed her over $3,000 in back support.

My reaction to Susan's request that I be her lawyer will illuminate the inquiry into how one pays for divorce-related problems. I had just opened my office and was concerned about making a living. Older country lawyers had given me fatherly advice, and the one thing on which they all agreed was that a lawyer must get his money in advance in criminal and domestic cases. Therefore, when Susan appeared I cold-bloodedly demanded $100 in advance. She wrote me a check, and we were off to squire's court.

My problem was to convert Bob's sojourn in jail into cash for Susan. This metamorphosis was not inevitable, because Bob didn't have any money. (The fact that a man stiffs his children does not mean that the money he saves is lying around for lawyers to appropriate.) Furthermore, Bob was being held on a misdemeanor criminal charge, which meant only that the state was going to exact a fine from him (which would go to the state) or impose a jail term on him. Susan was likely to get vindication but no money.

Under the nonsupport law, Bob was entitled to post a $500 appearance bond and get out of jail pending a full trial to decide whether he was guilty of nonsupport. I was sure that Bob would borrow bail money from his relatives and take off for Ohio. The bond would then be forfeited to the state.

Susan and I didn't care about prosecuting Bob. Furthermore, we were against diverting to the state any $500 he might lay his hands on. I suggested to both Bob and the layperson serving as justice of the peace (a common situation in many states) that if Bob would pay Susan the $500 Susan would move to dismiss the warrant and Bob could peacefully leave town.

Bob's relatives arrived with $500. Bob decided that it

was better to give the $500 to Susan than to the state, and we moved to dismiss the warrant. Susan netted $400 after deducting my $100 fee. That is not the end of the story, however. During the course of this long afternoon I had met Susan's children and saw how desperately poor the family was. And it was Christmas. I gave Susan back her check and told her I really hadn't had anything better to do that afternoon anyway (as I remember, an accurate representation).

I was by now incensed that Bob, who worked steadily in a high-paying job, did not support his children. There is a multistate compact known as the Uniform Reciprocal Enforcement of Support Act under which states agree to enforce the claims of one another's residents for support through the local prosecutors in the state where the defaulter resides. However, this scheme is a fiasco because prosecutors lack adequate staff, and retrieving support awards from voters for nonresidents is not a priority. So, rather than commit Susan's fate to the local prosecutor, I looked in the Cleveland lawyer directory and telephoned a young and hungry lawyer to whom I explained Susan's problem. I offered him one-half of everything he recovered for hounding Bob.

I offered half of the amount for a simple reason: unless working for Susan was profitable, he would be reluctant to take the case and work on it diligently. Over the next year Susan was entitled to $3,000, but the chances of collecting the whole $3,000 without considerable effort were remote. To get his fee the lawyer had to file an action in the Ohio general jurisdiction court, make an appearance, prepare a court order, and then collect Susan's money for her each month. If Bob defaulted on the Ohio court order, the lawyer would then be expected to have Bob put in jail until he paid. My offer induced the lawyer to take the case and do a good job. Susan started getting some money regularly.

There are millions of Susans, and her story illustrates just how expensive it is to collect the small sums of money that are usually involved in domestic awards. The amounts I presented are exact, although they reflect the value of the dollar in 1969. Today Susan's support payments would probably be double, but so would lawyers' fees. One point to keep in mind is that it is not much more expensive to go to court for $100,000 than it is for $100.

LAWYERS are regarded by adults about the way the Sheriff of Nottingham is regarded by children. Part of the general public's hostility comes from the fact that lawyers are expensive and have a monopoly on the use of courts. This is not the place to defend lawyers, but it is important for any discussion of how people pay for divorce to understand that private lawyers are businesspersons in a competitive market. Today, when law schools are turning out about thirty-five thousand new lawyers every year—almost half of whom cannot find jobs—the return from lawyering for most of the bar is only slightly better than the return from plumbing is to the average plumber. In 1982 the median income for lawyers was about $45,000 a year,[1] but that figure is deceptive. In the main, the lawyers with the six-

---

1. Earnings statistics for lawyers are hard to come by. I arrived at this figure on the basis of a 1980 Iowa study showing average earnings of private practitioners; a 1980 Bureau of Labor Statistics survey indicating average salaries at the starting level, at the top level, and four grades in between; and a survey of starting salaries compiled by *Student Lawyer* magazine. Readers who want more accurate figures can consult the IRS abstract on income, reported by occupations, which should be available by the time this book is published.

figure incomes who serve to beef up the average income figures are members of large firms that represent big business. Unless a client is very wealthy, these lawyers are not available to do routine domestic work.

Domestic law is largely the province of either government-supported legal services lawyers or general practitioners. Legal services lawyers are free to those who are poor enough to qualify. Although lawyers employed by legal services are usually competent and dedicated, they have a tremendous case load and can rarely give a client the type of individual attention a private lawyer can provide.

People who cannot qualify for legal services (the majority of those seeking divorces) are usually represented by general practitioners. Because these individuals handle the bulk of domestic matters, it is worthwhile to consider some of the professional, economic, and human tensions that make their job a difficult one.

Practicing law is demanding work. The body of law is enormous, and the law is different from state to state. Lawyers who practice domestic law do other types of general practice work as well; they are jacks-of-all-trades. It is much more difficult to practice general law than it is to be a specialist; moreover, this difficulty must be reflected to some degree in fees that reflect costs.

The economics of general practice does not allow a lawyer to take on a large volume of contested domestic cases. General practitioners work either alone or in small, two- to ten-person firms. They do not benefit from the high fees that big businesses are willing to pay and that make corporate practice lucrative. Yet they are faced with many of the same high overhead expenses.

Lawyers depend on expensive logistical support. They

must rent office space convenient to the courts, staff their offices, and provide themselves with a working library. Law books are expensive and must be updated annually either with replacement volumes or costly supplements; the yearly service charge on the small working law library of a solo practitioner approaches $2,500.

Air travel is expensive; postage is expensive; the telephone is expensive. Lawyers must take and pay for continuing legal education seminars that are often held out of town. A lawyer who is involved with government officials is expected to make political campaign contributions because that is how he or she sustains the goodwill necessary to get his or her clients' problems handled quickly.

Altman and Weil, a consulting firm for law office management, estimated in 1981 that in firms of between two and six lawyers the total overhead cost for each billable hour of lawyer time was slightly over $30. If the overhead in 1969 was half what it was in 1981, the six hours that I devoted to Susan's case cost me approximately $90.

At the time, I had nothing better to do. If I had intended to stay in private practice and keep creditors from baying at my door, however, that would have changed. I would have had to become very busy. Good trial lawyers must travel to interview witnesses and try cases far from home. They regularly make themselves available at night, on weekends, and even during vacations. All this is tolerable and perhaps even exhilarating, but it also strains physical stamina and causes problems at home where the demands of the job are always competing with the demands of domestic life.

Most smart people with law degrees, therefore, try to find an easier way to make a living: they join big firms, work for the government, or become employees of corporations. Lawyers who are willing to serve individual clients, are interested enough in their profession to work hard at it, and are smart enough to understand the whole system, are the lawyers whom everyone wants. Precisely because these lawyers get the business, they also gain experience, and they become better lawyers. The difference between these good lawyers and inexperienced or mediocre lawyers increases geometrically. When a person wants to hire such a lawyer, the fee reflects both the lawyer's skill and the arduousness of his or her life.

In assessing legal fees, it is important to remember that a portion of what the lawyer charges includes expenses of going to court that are entirely outside his or her control. All courts demand a filing fee to place a suit on the court's docket. Typically, this fee is about $20 in a state court, but in most states some type of waiver is available for indigent litigants. There is a fee for serving process, and in some jurisdictions contested divorces are heard by a court officer called a "special master" or "master of chancery" who is a practicing lawyer chosen by the judge to take testimony and make a report to the court. Usually the fee of the special master is borne by the litigants and can be more than $50 an hour. Appeals to higher courts involve the expense of typing and reproducing a transcript of the proceedings for the appellate court.

The "legal clinics" that have sprung up in the last ten years are one response to high legal costs. They are designed to serve the working and middle classes who cannot qualify for publicly supported legal aid. The legal clinic is usually staffed by young lawyers and is far less forbidding and mysterious than the general practitioner's office. In hospitality, the legal clinic is to a traditional lawyer's office what a small loan company is to a bank.

A legal clinic's fees are advertised in newspapers, and its offices are usually storefronts. For example, the Hyatt legal clinics located in the Washington, D.C., area often share office space with H & R Block, the tax company. The fall 1982 brochure for the Hyatt Legal Clinic provided these statements:

> Hyatt Legal Services charges $15 for an initial consultation, which is an opportunity for you to sit down with one of our attorneys to discuss your problem. Listed below is a sample schedule of our standard affordable fees for handling your legal problems . . .
>
> | | |
> |---|---|
> | Divorce, by Agreement | $250 |
> | Divorce, Uncontested | $350 |
> | Divorce, Contested | $650 |
>
> The above fees do not include court costs. Fees may be paid by cash or check. Hyatt Legal Services will provide more detailed fee information on request.

Several aspects of these cheap, affordable fees are worthy of attention. First, payment is expected in advance. Because going to court is usually an unbudgeted expense, most working-class domestic litigants have a hard time finding $250 to $650 to put up front. This is particularly true for women, many of whom are dependent on their husbands for their spending money. Yet it is cheaper in terms of overhead for a law office to do business on a cash-in-advance basis—there are no bad debts. These savings can be passed on to the consumer in the same way that a cash-and-carry discount store passes on savings in the form of low prices.

The Hyatt fee schedule specifically excludes court costs, and although it does not mention them, appeals require another fee. Finally, the category of "contested divorce" that is priced at $650 probably contemplates a one-day trial that produces a court order divorcing the parties, awarding the property, and establishing the custody of children. It does not contemplate any further proceedings to collect alimony, change custody, or enforce visitation rights. Thus, it would appear that in the Washington, D.C., area in 1982 the rock-bottom price for a contested divorce without unusual complications was $1,300 ($650 each for husband and wife) plus about $100 in miscellaneous court costs. Fourteen hundred dollars is a big chunk of a middle-class family's yearly after-tax income; it is prohibitively expensive for the bottom 30 percent of American families, which is why we have created publicly funded legal aid.

Legal clinics may be an attractive alternative for some, but they are not the answer to everyone's prayers. In my view, the real hero of the American legal process remains the small-firm general practitioner who, contrary to popular belief, is not a lightning-fast calculator of his or her own best economic interests. Although there are lazy, greedy, and incompetent lawyers that hold themselves out as general practitioners, they are a minority, and they prosper only in proportion to public ignorance of their reputations. The lawyers who have most of the business are usually generous and often represent a surprising number of domestic clients whose legal affairs end up costing the lawyer money.

Many lawyers enjoy applying their craft to the relief of suffering. Although it would be unrealistic to pretend that lawyers think first and foremost of public service rather than of their own livelihoods, abject cynicism is not called for. In my own experience, the reason that domestic relations litigation gets done at all for people like Susan, who could not possibly pay for a lawyer on a reasonable hourly basis, is that lawyers do more free work than plumbers, electricians, garage mechanics, or unionized auto workers. General practice lawyers organize their practice so that well-heeled clients subsidize the Susans of this world. Even today, with government-supported legal aid, Susan would not be eligible for a free lawyer.

The general practice lawyer will often take a domestic client on credit, a practice indispensable for many women because they have no money. As a natural outgrowth of a husband's traditional duty to support his wife, a husband must pay his wife's lawyer if she files for divorce. Few husbands, however, are willing to fork over lawyers' fees for a divorce proceeding in the same casual way that they provide grocery money. This protection of woman's legal rights is a nullity unless a lawyer is willing to file the initial papers on credit so that the wife can get a court order requiring her husband to pay him.

Court orders to pay lawyers do not have the same effect on a lawyer's balance sheet as cash in advance does, however: enforcing fee awards is like pulling teeth. As often as not, the husband refuses to honor the court order, which means that the lawyer must go through more court rigmarole to put the husband in jail until he comes up with the money, assuming that the husband has the money. If the husband has no money or borrowing power, the lawyer might as well paper his bathroom with his court order. In fact, of all routine law practice, domestic cases present the greatest bad-debt problem, and this problem must be figured into all domestic case fees as a cost of handling that type of case.

In general practice, big money is earned when big money changes hands. Legal fees in routine types of cases like divorce are resented by clients because they are unbudgeted and only confer benefits to which the clients feel entitled anyway. When big money changes hands, however, clients who receive new money are less grudging about paying their lawyers. If Great-Uncle Peter dies leaving us an unexpected $100,000, paying $10,000 for estate administration hardly hurts at all. If our automobile accident case is settled for $150,000—roughly three times what we expected—it does not hurt to give our lawyer a third of that settlement. Even when we borrow $150,000 to buy a house, it does not hurt to borrow another $2,000 to pay the lawyers for the closing costs and title search—the difference over twenty-five years is a few dollars a month.

When I was practicing law, I never charged a domestic client for giving advice unless he or she insisted on paying me. In fact, I sent many women who wanted divorces to social service agencies because they could not care for their children if they lost the support of their husbands. Sometimes mental health services and church counseling worked and sometimes they didn't, but I gave my clients the best advice I could regardless of whether that encouraged them to use and pay for my services. I was able to give this kind of advice and not starve only because I was subsidized by rich corporate clients, labor unions, fat estates, and accident victims.

Domestic work generates goodwill, brings in other clients with fee-paying work, and helps meet fixed costs during slack periods. If a team of business school professors investigated the economics of domestic practice, however, they would probably conclude that contested divorce cases are financial albatrosses. (Uncontested cases, where the lawyer only files the papers, reduces a settlement agreement to writing, and gets a court order, produce a reasonable profit.)

Not only do divorce cases generate red ink; they also are time-consuming because the lawyer must double as counselor and confidant. Since general practice lawyers can handle contested domestic work only because of fees generated by other clients, they cannot afford to be blithely reassuring when full-fee-paying business is making countervailing demands on their time. It is understandable that clients going through a period of trauma expect their attorneys to stand by their side, but experienced practitioners realize that today's crisis is only another inevitable step along a seemingly endless road. If lawyers are to be there when they can actually do some good, they must leave some of the hand holding to others while they go about the mundane routine of making a living.

The divorce process is usually seen either as an exercise in arranging a negotiated settlement or as a one-shot courtroom encounter that gives an order disposing of all issues. In fact, statistics would lead us to conclude that most divorces involve nothing but a settlement. In Los Angeles County in 1982, for example, over 92 percent of all divorce cases were concluded by an agreed order. Most of the remaining 8 percent were handled satisfactorily through California's mandatory pretrial mediation process, and only a small percentage demanded the intrusion of the trial court judge. If working out an agreement or going to court for a day took care of most domestic matters, there would be no great problem about paying for divorce or getting lawyers to handle divorces expeditiously. But, as usual, the statistics are misleading.

Settlement is frequently the result of litigant exhaustion after numerous preliminary court battles. When a family breaks up, passions run hot. There are the preliminary questions of who should move out of the home, how the children should be supported during divorce proceedings, and who will pay the wife's bills during the transition. If a couple have been relatively civilized in talking through their divorce plans, these questions may be worked out in advance. If a husband beats his wife and she takes refuge in a lawyer's office, however, all these questions must be answered by a court. Often, therefore, a divorce proceeding is begun, not only by filing a divorce complaint, but also by a motion for a temporary injunction requiring the husband to move out, pay child support, pay the wife's attorney's fees, and pay temporary support for the wife as well. Bringing such a motion to court may take a full day of a lawyer's time. If the order is resisted, the lawyer will be involved in hearings to get coercive orders covering temporary matters before the final hearing on divorce is even scheduled.

Once both parties get a taste of courtroom proceedings, they may conclude that they should listen to their lawyers and come to a peaceful agreement about property division, alimony, child support, and custody. This leads to the preparation of a settlement order resolving all these matters and places the case in the ''settled-before-trial'' pigeonhole. That categorization is misleading not only because it ignores preliminary proceedings before a divorce is awarded; it is misleading also because it ignores further proceedings, often seemingly countless in number, to modify the terms of a divorce decree after a divorce has been awarded.

Court-ordered child custody, visitation rights, child support, and alimony are all terms of a divorce decree that a court can modify any time there is a significant change of circumstances. If a woman remarries, a man can go back to court to relitigate all the terms of child custody and support. If a man loses his job, a child gets sick, or inflation increases the cost of living, a court can reevaluate its initial decree with respect to alimony, child support, and even custody.

It is important to understand the breadth of a domestic court's powers. If people are quarreling violently but do not want to file for divorce, a domestic court can intervene in a matter of hours to prevent physical violence. In a matter of days the court can give temporary relief concerning child custody, determine use of jointly owned property like the house or car, and even order the husband to provide support money for the wife and children. Although it is usually more convenient to bring these types of issues to a domestic court in the form of a request for temporary relief pending a divorce action, it need not be done that way if the quarreling parties either oppose divorce on principle or just do not want to go that far at the moment.

THE way divorce courts work is probably best illustrated by example. One of the remarkable aspects of domestic cases is their repetitive nature. Three cases in court this week will be almost indistinguishable from three cases next week. There are, for example, peaceful and amicable divorces where the parties sincerely try to do right by each other and the children. There are comparatively peaceful divorces that are characterized, nonetheless, by very hard bargaining on one or both sides. Finally, there are violent divorces characterized by verbal and often physical abuse. Among working- and middle-class Americans the property fights almost always involve the same issues—use of the jointly owned family home; who gets the car, furniture, appliances, and housewares; the level of alimony (if any) and child support; and the allocation of the family's jointly acquired debt.

The hypothetical case that I am about to describe is best understood as a "composite"; George and Alice are similar in every regard to hundreds of divorce litigants who have had cases before me in the last twelve years. The level of violence in their family, their immaturity, their comparative poverty, the competitive inequities in their positions, and their relationships with their parents and their children are typical of millions of couples.

George and Alice are twenty-seven and twenty-three years old, respectively. They live in the small southeastern city of Treeville where George earns $17,000 a year as a city police officer and Alice earns $6,500 as a retail store clerk. George has had two years of college (taken at night through a police department grant) at Treeville Junior College, and Alice is a high school graduate who did well in the commerce program. Being a police officer exposes George to many women, and he frequently succumbs to temptation. Alice is no paragon of virtue either, and she is equally open to an occasional casual affair.

George and Alice have two children, a three-year-old boy and an eighteen-month-old girl, both of whom are looked after during the day by Alice's mother, who lives across the street. George and Alice don't like each other very well, and they fight over money constantly. Although Alice does most of the physical child care when the children are not at her mother's, George is arguably the better parent because he sacrifices more of his discretionary leisure time to give the children high-quality attention.

Violent daily quarrels characterize the household: Alice has on occasion attacked George with a knife, and George has been known to slap Alice around, though never badly enough to do any serious damage. One day, however, George picks Alice up and heaves her out the door with the admonition that if she returns he will "kick her ass up between her shoulder blades." Alice goes to her parents; George stays in the house with the children. The next day is a Sunday, and Alice returns expecting George to have cooled. But George has not cooled and takes off his belt with every intention of doing some real damage to Alice. Alice again flees to her parents' house.

The next day George must report to work. Since no alternative to the normal arrangement for child care is available, George takes the children across the street and presents them to their grandmother without comment. When George returns from work, he goes at once to get the children. At this point, he is surprised by Alice's father who aims a double-barreled shotgun at George and says he will "blow George away" if George so much as touches the screen door. Thus develops a Mexican standoff that goes on for several days with tempers getting hotter.

George wants to see his children, and because George is a police officer, a lot of his friends are lawyers. Furthermore, because police officers often help lawyers, lawyers in small towns tend not to charge police officers for routine services. George approaches one of his lawyer friends, who advises him that he can either begin a divorce proceeding and petition for temporary custody of the children or he can use the remedy of habeas corpus to get a court order allowing him to see his children. George decides that he wants a divorce anyway, so his lawyer files for divorce and, at the same time, asks the court for a temporary order giving George custody of the children.

Three days later George and Alice are before the judge. Alice, who has no money, has found a young lawyer to represent her on credit until the court orders George to pay her legal fees. The judge is sympathetic to George's desire to see his children, but he finds George's overall treatment of Alice less than acceptable. Furthermore, the judge finds that during the divorce proceeding the children will be better off if they continue to live with their mother and grandparents. Therefore, the judge orders that pending divorce Alice has exclusive use of the house and temporary custody of the children (subject to George's reasonable visitation rights); the judge also orders George to pay $300 a month support for Alice and the children and another $500 for her attorney. George gets to keep the family car because Alice can use her parents' car when necessary.

George has just been bankrupted. He must find a place to live, buy a television set and a few sticks of furniture, and find $500 for Alice's lawyer. George doesn't have $500, and since he is already heavily in debt, he cannot borrow the money. Alice's lawyer, however, agrees to take $50 a month, and he considers himself lucky. The lawyers on each side begin to bang out the type of compromise that is routine in cases of this sort.

Although George is a good father in that he enjoys

spending time with the children, it is not practical to award him custody. The reason has nothing to do with Alice's superior ability as a parent, but rather with Alice's parents. Since both George and Alice work full time—necessarily given their economic circumstances—the children have spent more waking hours with their grandparents than with both of their parents combined. Although George knows that Alice and her parents will disparage him to the children if Alice retains custody, he has no alternative, since he has no free-of-charge surrogate available to care for the children all day.

It is agreed, therefore, that Alice gets the children subject to George's right to take them whenever he wants. Although Alice's parents would like to limit the children's exposure to George, Alice is glad for George to take the children so that she can have the weekends free. Alice is allowed to have exclusive use of their jointly owned house until the children are eighteen, and George's alimony is limited to the mortgage payment of $285 per month, plus the taxes and insurance. In addition, George must pay $200 a month child support.

George keeps the car, but Alice gets most of the furniture. Neither George nor Alice is particularly satisfied with this arrangement. Alice thinks that she is entitled to more money, and George thinks that Alice should have to pay half the mortgage and give him half the furniture. Nevertheless, George and Alice finally settle because the lawyers advise them that this agreement is about what a court would decide. Litigation would be unavailing and expensive. Accordingly, an agreed court order is entered that divorces the parties and that reflects the property settlement and the custody arrangement.

Up until this point George and Alice have had a pretty cheap divorce. George's lawyer friend did not charge him at all, and Alice's lawyer agreed to be paid in installments. There were court costs of about $100. This initial negotiated settlement and court order, however, may be only the beginning of a legal battle that can intrude into everyone's life for the next fifteen years.

What happens, for example, if Alice's parents continue to despise George and make it difficult for him to visit his children? Here is a typical scenario: George is forced to change shifts, so that he gets two days off in the middle of the week but has to work weekends. Alice's mother says that weekday visitation is unreasonable because of the children's nursery school schedule, but George cannot visit them on weekends. George must now go to court for an order clarifying his visitation rights, and doing this, unless he again imposes on his lawyer friend, will cost about $150. Alice or her parents must hire a lawyer to answer George's petition, and this time, since George is right, Alice will have to pay for her lawyer.

As time passes both Alice and George will look for new companionship. Alice marries an unemployed factory worker whose only income is a small monthly disability check from the Veterans Administration; George marries a schoolteacher. George is probably now in a better position than Alice to bring up the children.

Remarriage opens up almost limitless possibilities for litigation. Frequently children do not like their stepparents, and when they visit their noncustodial natural parent they may tell real or fabricated horror stories about how their stepparents and stepparents' relatives treat them. Such stories understandably arouse justified bitterness on the part of the noncustodial natural parent and frequently lead to efforts to change custody.

Noncustodial parents, however, often use the remarriage of their former spouses as an excuse to relitigate the whole issue of custody, and if people have money and are willing to spend it, they can hire the same type of expert witnesses to testify about psychological phenomena that they might have hired in the original divorce proceeding. If the noncustodial parent is in the superior financial position, the custodial parent may be subjected to a serious financial drain. Fortunately, domestic courts have broad powers to require payment in advance of the other party's attorney's fee before considering such motions to change custody, but whether a court uses such powers is discretionary with the judge. The lawyer must be willing to take a poor party's case on credit in order to make a motion before the court for an attorney's fee award.

In the case of Alice's new husband, however, George's concern for his children's welfare is justified. Although George never liked Alice's parents, he acknowledged that Alice's mother was a good caretaker who treated his children as if they were her own. Alice's new husband is another matter. George thinks he should now have custody because, with his new wife, he will give the children a better environment than Alice and her husband can give them. The tension concerning the children is complicated by the fact that Alice was no longer eligible for alimony when she remarried. George sees no reason why he should continue to pay the mortgage on a house for Alice and her new husband; he wants the house sold and the proceeds divided between them.

Alice and her parents want Alice to retain custody of the children. It is Alice's mother who is the most emotional

and militant, however. She hopes that everyone will understand that the children are really *hers* because she has invested five years of daily love rearing them. Furthermore,
she is not alone; the children feel the same way. Alice, for
her part, believes that the so-called alimony of providing
money for the house was really child support. If George is
allowed to have the house sold and the proceeds divided,
Alice thinks that his cash support for the children should
be increased. So when George hires a lawyer to get custody
and a court order allowing the sale of the house, Alice's
lawyer files a cross action to increase child support.

All these issues could, of course, be settled just as those
in the initial divorce were. The highly emotional issue of
the children's custody, however, makes that course unlikely because now no compromise is possible. This conflict
requires an all-or-nothing call by a neutral judge.

Litigating these issues will be complicated. In this new
proceeding the court is asked to determine the effect of
Alice's new husband on the children. Does Alice's new
husband drink to excess? If so, how does he conduct himself when drinking? How does he relate to the children? Do
the children like him? At the same time, however, the judge
must also ask: What type of a person is George's new wife?
How do the children like her? Where do the children want
to live?

Regardless of how these matters are decided, the lawyers' fees on each side will be between $500 and $1,000, to
which the inevitable court costs will be added. If experts
are hired, they too must be paid. Furthermore, this is the
type of case that justifies an appeal by whichever side loses.
Chalk up another $500 to $1,000 per side for the appeal in a
reasonably cheap jurisdiction.

This part of George and Alice's story corresponds

closely to a real case decided in West Virginia in 1982. As I have presented it, the chances of each side's winning are fifty-fifty, and in fact, the real case on which it is based was so close that the trial court judge called me to determine whether the state supreme court had any recent but unpublished decisions on child custody that might instruct his decision. The real judge wanted to give the children to George, and George presented a strong case. After looking at both sides, however, a judge might just as well decide that more damage would be done to the children by changing their living arrangements after patterns have been firmly established.

More to the point, a discerning judge is likely to be impressed by the fact that Alice's mother has been the actual caretaker and is the individual involved in this whole mess most worthy of court sympathy. Let us assume, therefore, that George loses his bid to change custody. To make matters worse for George, let us also assume that the court accepts Alice's argument that part of her alimony was really child support and increases George's cash payments from $200 to $400 per month, although George is allowed to sell the house.

George is understandably outraged. In fact, he is so outraged that he decides to move elsewhere and to forget about his first family. Because George is an experienced police officer with college training, his job prospects are comparatively bright. His new wife's job prospects are equally promising. George and his wife move to Florida, where George's police experience guarantees him instant employment on a village police force. Alice stays in Treeville with her husband, her accommodating parents, her growing children, and her mediocre job. She cannot make it without the $400 a month child support (tax free), but now there is little chance of George paying it.

When George was in Treeville he always paid the mortgage, and although he did not always come up with his $200 promptly, he paid about 90 percent of what he owed. Now, however, he has placed himself at sufficient geographical remove just to stop paying. In Florida he rents a little apartment, puts all his property in his wife's name, and spends whatever money comes his way.

If Alice can find a young, competent, and hungry Florida lawyer to bring action in a Florida court to get a Florida support order, and thereafter enforce that order with threats of jail for contempt of court, she might get some money. The problem is that Alice, like most domestic litigants, has no idea of how to do this. If she goes to a local lawyer, he or she will probably charge her for subcontracting to a Florida lawyer. Furthermore, the local lawyer may or may not pick the right lawyer in Florida for such work. Although it is theoretically possible to enforce support without paying more than a third to lawyers when the defaulter has a regular salary, in practice it usually does not work that way.[2]

Another option for Alice is to go to the prosecuting attorney (sometimes called the district attorney) of Treeville and request assistance under the Uniform Reciprocal Enforcement of Support Act. This is the statute I mentioned earlier that facilitates the collection of delinquent

---

2. Alice can also wait until the arrears amount to $5,000 and then bring suit. But if she tries that approach she will be in the same circumstances as my own client, Susan, was because George will have spent her $400 a month, and it will be almost impossible to collect her lump-sum judgment. If Alice goes to the trouble of finding a lawyer and filing a complaint, she'll probably compromise her $5,000 claim and settle for $1,000 in cash plus her lawyer's fee.

alimony and child support across state lines. Under this act, the prosecuting attorney in the county where the recipient of the support is located files papers with the prosecuting attorney of the out-of-state county where the defaulting party lives. The prosecuting attorney of the defaulter's state then brings an action in the local trial court to enforce the foreign support decree. Occasionally this procedure works well, but in my experience and the experience of prosecutors across the country, the occasions are few and far between.

The reasons are manifold. First, the recipient of support must know where the defaulting party is. Special statutes now allow the federal government to help local authorities track down support defaulters through Social Security records, but a formal request from a local government agency is required to obtain this information. Second, even when the defaulter is located, two unlikely conditions must co-exist before the person who needs the support will receive any money. The prosecuting attorney's office in the demanding jurisdiction must be efficient, and the prosecuting attorney's office in the defaulter's jurisdiction must be efficient. If both of these conditions are met, a few dollars may be recovered. Even then, however, the defaulter can hire a lawyer who is usually able to strain the thin resources allocated to handling these cases to the point where proceedings grind to a halt.

Prosecuting attorneys are overworked and understaffed. Not only are their offices responsible for prosecuting all local crimes, juvenile delinquency, and child neglect but in most places prosecutors are the lawyers for numerous government agencies as well. Prosecuting attorneys do not have enough lawyers to do any of these tasks well, and practical politics demands that the collection of delinquent support for out-of-state beneficiaries be relegated to a low priority. The federal government has found incompetence and understaffing such a problem in collecting money for families on welfare that it now hires assistant prosecuting attorneys and assistant state attorneys general itself. This federally funded program gives prosecutors and attorneys general staff whose only job is the collection of support for the *federal government* with no charge to their local budgets, but these employees prosecute only those defaulters whose former families are on welfare.

When a state welfare department steps in and pays the support for a defaulter, the defaulter then owes the welfare department that money. The federal government is interested because the budgets of state welfare departments come mostly from federal grants. Ironically, then, the least urgent need for prosecution occurs when the family is being supported by welfare. The critical point here is that the federal government itself recognizes that if collection is to be done by a public agency competent personnel must be hired and paid from a source other than local budgets.

In order to double-check my experience regarding interstate support enforcement, I called several local prosecutors' offices. These officers agreed that when they send papers to other states they collect money in only 10 percent of the cases. When papers are sent to them from elsewhere, they admit that they collect money only when the defaulter goes along more or less voluntarily. Furthermore, the existence of an out-of-state order for a certain sum does not mean that the court in the defaulter's home state will order that same amount paid. The local court can make an inde-

pendent determination of the defaulter's ability to pay before ordering any payment.[3]

The routine procedure for prosecuting attorneys when
collecting support for out-of-state beneficiaries is to send a
letter to the defaulter telling him or her to appear in court.
If he or she does not appear, another letter is sent. If the
person still does not appear, the case is dropped. Prosecutors confess that they do not have the staff to arrest defaulters and haul them before the court. Once a person appears,
however, the judge will order him or her to pay a reasonable sum to the court clerk. If money is not paid, the prosecutor waits for notification from the demanding state
before initiating new proceedings. There is usually no direct contact between the court clerk who collects the
money and the prosecutor. If Alice decides to pursue
George through her local prosecutor's office, the chances
are about 90 percent that she will never see a cent, particularly since George will have the same type of lawyer
friends in Florida that he had in Treeville.

The most efficient way to enforce a support award is to
put the defaulter in jail until he or she pays. A few hours in
jail usually inspires an urge to be accommodating. There is,
however, a limit to this technique; people cannot be put in
jail until they pay unless they are *able* to pay. If the defaulter does not have the money and cannot borrow it or
sell assets, he or she cannot be jailed for not paying. Furthermore, an out-of-state defaulter cannot be placed in an

3. As a technical matter, this is true because support payments are not the
result of "final judgments" by a court; they are subject to revision in changed
circumstances. If the party not receiving support gets a formal court judgment for
the amount of the arrears, however, another state's court would have to honor
that final judgment under the "full faith and credit" clause of the United States
Constitution.

out-of-state jail without a support order from a court in that state.

In George's case, until there is a Florida court order requiring him to pay, he cannot be in contempt of a Florida court and therefore cannot be placed in a Florida jail. If George owes Alice $5,000, chances are that by the time she finally tracks him down George won't be able to raise $5,000 to save his soul. All Alice will get is an unenforceable Florida court judgment for $5,000 against George and a local order reaffirming his obligation to pay her $400 a month. For complicated technical legal reasons Alice cannot use the threat of jail to enforce her judgment for the $5,000 in back support. She can use it, however, to get her $400 a month, or whatever the Florida court orders, in the future.

Because George does not own any property, Alice cannot collect her judgment immediately, but she can attach his wages, in which event she might get as much as $400 a month in *back support*. Even if Alice hires a diligent local lawyer to harry George like the Furies, a Florida court may nonetheless conclude that, given George's circumstances, $400 a month is too much. If the Florida court thinks that $400 is beyond George's capacity to pay, it will enforce through contempt only the payment that it thinks is reasonable. Since, in general, defaulters are voting residents of the jurisdictions where the support must be enforced, and since local judges are often elected, a certain amount of judicial home cooking is not entirely unheard of in these matters.

This presentation is only a rough outline, since the rules concerning enforcement are different in every state and some places are more efficient than others. The point is not the exact procedure by which support can be collected but, rather, the speculative nature of collecting support from mobile people. If public officials are entrusted to collect support, their incentive to do it diligently is negligible; if private lawyers are hired to collect it, they will siphon off between one-third and one-half of what they collect in lawyers' fees. The conclusion is that if George moves across the country Alice is better off agreeing to take $200 a month regularly in return for leaving George in peace than she is in trying to get all the money to which she is entitled. Once again, the innocent children suffer.

Child-snatching by the noncustodial parent is another common problem, and it raises the most heated passions between domestic litigants. When child-snatching occurs, most general practice lawyers (although probably not the legal clinics) will file the appropriate papers in court without demanding an up-front payment if they handled the original divorce. In these circumstances, getting paid at all is chancy, so fast and efficient service can hardly be expected. Of course, if a client is a doctor or a business executive with money in the bank, he or she can retain a large firm with numerous young lawyers available at all hours of the day and night to provide immediate service. Domestic work for the rich is done quickly and enthusiastically. Big firms, however, charge between $75 and $200 an hour for their lawyers' time, depending on the experience of the lawyer, and a reasonable bill from such firms for making a motion about child custody is in the neighborhood of $500.

This brings me to a concluding observation about transactional costs and justice. I tend to speak positively about general practitioners who do domestic work on a subsidized basis. However, the fact that many lawyers do such subsidized work for some clients part of the time does not mean that a person in trouble can always find such a lawyer. Usually, unless the lawyer has done business with the client before, he or she will want to be paid in advance. Even a lawyer who is philosophical about helping his clients through a year of "shake-out" litigation over custody, visitation, or support eventually gets worn out if the parties don't quiet down in a reasonable period.

Ordinarily, if a party to a domestic matter is in a superior financial position and invites litigation, he or she will be required to pay the other side's lawyer—often even if he or she wins. Yet here again a lawyer for a poor domestic litigant must do a lot of work before the lawyer knows whether he or she will actually get paid by the other side. If lawyers are young and hungry, they may have nothing better to do than to take such speculative cases; that is how they gain experience and a reputation. They may not be the best lawyers for a serious case, but the best lawyers already have more full-fee-paying work than they can handle. When a good lawyer who has no particular sympathy for Alice realizes that to be paid at all he will need to squeeze his fee out of someone like George, the lawyer is likely to require payment in advance. The lawyer will then repay Alice if George coughs up. If Alice or her parents cannot come up with the advance money, Alice is effectively foreclosed from asserting her claims.

As I suggest in the concluding chapter, there are some across-the-board reforms that would help this situation. The simplest reform is to require all support money to be paid to a public officer in the county where the payor lives. It would be the officer's duty automatically to take defaulters to court if payment were not received by the tenth of the month. An adequately staffed service of this type could be funded from a mere 5 percent of all collected support awards. It would be cheap at four times the price. Possibly the most important effect would be hidden—a higher number of voluntary payments would be made as the prospect of effective enforcement would make use of the enforcement service unnecessary.

Child custody and visitation rights present a more thorny problem. There is little alternative to the current system of privately borne costs when parents want to argue about custody. Any publicly supported scheme would encourage unmanageable litigation, since human conflict about children is potentially limitless. No matter how many lawyers might be publicly employed to fight custody battles, demand would exceed supply. A private price system is necessary to ration scarce resources. The expenses of enforcing visitation rights or of getting a child returned from a party who has illegally taken the child, however, should be handled by a court agency funded from the same charge against support awards. There is a big difference between litigation designed to change existing court orders and litigation designed to enforce court orders that have already been entered.

Because the divorced household is becoming as much the norm as the married household, it is time to give some thought to reducing the private transactional costs of collecting support. Mechanisms that spread these transactional costs over society as a whole, along the lines of other social insurance programs, are overdue in a society where half the parents with young children to support are likely to be divorced. Alice is entitled to support for her children. More to the point, although the trial court may have been wrong in not granting George's petition to modify custody, once custody was left with Alice, the children were entitled to enough money to be able to live in a decent place, buy clothes and school supplies, and have some spare change for a little recreation.

It is the very inefficiency of collecting support that encourages defaulters. Numerous empirical studies have shown that the lack of effective enforcement, not financial inability, causes people to ignore support orders.[4] A good nationwide, self-financing system for collecting support would discourage people from fleeing and would make court action to collect support necessary less often. Although I cannot resist describing how things can be done better, there are strong political forces that want things left exactly the way they are.[5] For the foreseeable future the domestic litigant must anticipate an incompetent system.

Anyone who is currently contemplating divorce should recognize that enforcing any aspect of a divorce decree—including such an absolute as the placement of children—is at best speculative. When, for example, a child is taken across the country by a parent who does not have court-ordered custody, it costs the custodial parent thousands of dollars in legal fees and travel expenses to retrieve the child. Although states have passed statutes almost guaranteeing that the child will be returned to the custodial parent, enforcing these statutes against a recalcitrant kidnapper costs more money than most people can afford.

Earlier chapters of this book suggested why court-

---

4. Two such studies are David Chambers's *Making Fathers Pay*, which drew upon empirical data collected in Michigan, and a California study by Lenore Wietzman on "The Economics of Divorce: Social and Economic Consequences of Property, Alimony and Child Support Awards," *U.C.L.A. Law Review*, 28 (1981).

5. I have devoted an entire book to the exploration of this proposition. See *Why Courts Don't Work* (New York: McGraw-Hill, 1983).

devised divorce settlements can never satisfy the parties. But even those imperfect arrangements paint too bright a picture. A woman who needs $1,000 a month to support her three children will be forced to settle for $600. As if that were not bad enough, she may have to spend $200 of that to assure payment of the rest, and even this sacrifice may be unavailing. Former husbands must either support two households or reconcile themselves to constant court battles and regular flight to avoid judicial process.

Divorce not only leaves both parties economically and emotionally poorer, it also strikes at our sense of continuity and stability. It is hard to establish a budget if next month's check doesn't come. It is hard to create a stable environment for children if a weekend visit turns into a three-month captivity. The law says those things *should* not happen, but it can not assure that they *do* not.

5

When to Hire a Lawyer, When to Go to Court, and When to Settle

THE market is glutted with books about how to get a divorce without a lawyer. The popularity of these books and the increasing use in many jurisdictions of standard forms that can be completed by laypersons on their own behalf for no-fault divorces testify both to the high cost of lawyers and to individuals' reluctance to part with what little money they have for a commodity that is as intangible as legal advice. People resent paying large legal fees and prefer a do-it-yourself approach whenever possible. We do the same thing in health care; few of us go to a doctor to cure a cold. When, however, what we at first thought was a cold turns into pneumonia, we usually decide that it is time for professional help. Unfortunately, in divorce there is no telltale sign like a high fever to alert us that we need more than a home remedy.

The people who are least likely to retain good lawyers to help them with their divorces are the people who expect "amicable" settlements. Yet, because all settlement negotiations either are or should be conducted in the shadow of what the law entitles people to, it is self-defeating to discuss settlement terms with even the most agreeable spouse without a definite idea about what a judge would probably give a person in court and about the future legal consequences of the terms of any settlement.

A lawyerless divorce is probably as good as any for young, childless couples who have been married a short time. Usually there is no valuable property to be divided, no issue of child custody, and no question of continuing support by one party for the other. If husband and wife decide that they just want out—he'll take the television set and she'll take the silver—there isn't much reason to hire lawyers if there are easily understood do-it-yourself forms available.

When a couple have been married for several years and have children, however, it is important for the parties to understand exactly what they are doing. Domestic law is full of procedural technicalities. Certain words in a court order have specific meanings, and those meanings imply definite—and often surprising—legal consequences. A person can be locked into a bad bargain for the rest of his or her life merely because some inappropriate phrase was used in a settlement agreement or certain magic-formula words were omitted from a final court order.

For example, it makes an enormous difference to both parties whether a woman is awarded no alimony or alimony of one dollar a year.[1] If a court decree provides for no alimony, a woman is forever barred from going back to court to get help from her former husband if she loses her

---

1. Of course, some men receive alimony from their ex-wives. But it is rare.

job, gets sick, or otherwise falls on hard times. However, if a woman receives alimony of only one dollar a year, she can go back to court to request an increase if her circumstances change for the worse. Often even when a wife can support her accustomed standard of living from her own job, a court will still allow "nominal" alimony. The purpose of the nominal award is to leave open the possibility of giving real alimony later if necessary. Obviously, an award of nominal alimony constitutes a significant contingent liability for a man; conversely, it constitutes a valuable insurance policy for a woman.

In a similar vein, how a court order characterizes a man's payments to his former wife is extremely important. Child support automatically stops when children reach the age of eighteen unless the law of a particular state authorizes the courts to provide for advanced education. Alimony, on the other hand, continues until a former wife dies or remarries. Alimony is taxable to the wife and is a tax deduction for the husband; child support is neither a tax deduction for the husband nor taxable to the wife. If the husband pays more than 50 percent of a child's support, he is entitled to the standard personal income tax exemption for the child.

Under federal tax law, if a court awards "periodic payments" that include both alimony and child support but makes no allocation between the two, the entire amount is a tax deduction to the husband and is taxable to the wife. Usually this scheme saves taxes, making more money available for everyone concerned because the wife is more often in the lower tax bracket. With periodic payments, however, a husband is never sure how much the payment will be reduced when a child turns eighteen. An advance allocation between alimony and child support in a court order providing for periodic payments will defeat the favorable tax consequences of just calling the award "periodic payments," but if ten years after the initial decree a court decides that most of the periodic payment was alimony and not child support, the man may end up paying what he thought was child support until his children are half a century old.

Usually an alimony award stops when the husband dies, but in most states a court can specifically provide in its divorce order that alimony will be a charge against a former husband's estate. This can be an important provision if the husband is older than his wife and has accumulated enough property so that his estate will be able to satisfy a claim for continuing support. The justification for permitting alimony to be a charge against an estate is that, if the parties had stayed married, the wife would have been entitled to at least one-third of her husband's estate at his death and thus would have had continuing support.

Considerations such as these constitute yet another reason why settlement is often preferable to a litigated divorce. Problems like the allocation of tax benefits, insurance to substitute for alimony if a man dies, and the amount by which payments will be reduced when children are emancipated can be handled better by well-drafted contracts than they can by standard court orders. For example, periodic payments can be so much for the first twelve years, so much for the next five years, and then so much forever after. Such a contract combines the favorable tax treatment of periodic payments with the certainty that the man's financial obligation will be reduced when his children are emancipated. Factors such as inflation or the income of the party making the periodic payments can also be taken into account, and a formula to adjust automatically for changes in either can be stipulated in the agreement. By providing for the purchase of an insurance policy on the husband's life, such a contract can even handle quite neatly the eventuality of death.

Most jurisdictions will honor fair settlement agreements. Theoretically, courts examine proposed settlements to determine whether they are indeed fair, but, as I pointed out before, crowded dockets often mean that the review is perfunctory. Once a court concludes by its order that a settlement is fair, however, it can make that settlement the final and immutable resolution of a couple's marriage. Exactly how this is done involves some of the most complicated aspects of divorce law, and the penalties for doing it unskillfully are often draconian.

W HAT follows is complicated, but its purpose is to demonstrate that do-it-yourself lawyering can be as dangerous as do-it-yourself brain surgery. Although I have simplified as much as possible, a somewhat detailed discussion of legal technicalities is necessary to explain just how complicated domestic law can become and why professional advice is needed if there is anything at all at stake.

Much of the law's technical complexity is designed to permit careful and deliberate engineering by knowledgeable draftsmen. The law is structured on the presumption that lawyers understand the technicalities and that they will draft their agreements with those technicalities in mind. Technicalities become a way of tailoring an agreement so that it exactly embodies the understandings of the parties.

When laypersons try to do the work of lawyers, that presumption is not justified, but laypersons are just as bound by the language they use in their contracts as are lawyers. The difference is that lawyers know what certain words mean to courts, whereas laypersons do not.

It must be understood first of all that a divorce court is a court of *equity*. That talismanic term implies certain powers peculiar to divorce courts. It is always a nightmare to explain satisfactorily the difference between courts of law and courts of equity. Even law students are confounded by the distinction because the separate rules that surround equity are entirely the product of history rather than of science. In eighteenth-century England, equity courts and law courts were different entities with different judges and different jurisdictions. In twentieth-century America the same judge often hears both law cases and equity cases; today the difference between whether a case will be heard according to the rules of law or the rules of equity depends on which courts in England would have heard the matter at the time of the American Revolution.

For example, matters involving crimes, breaches of contract and personal injuries were always heard in courts of law, while matters involving trusts and estates were always heard in courts of equity. Courts of law gave jury trials; courts of equity did not give jury trials. Today, if an action is equitable rather than legal, the litigants are not entitled to a jury. There is no reasoned justification for the distinction, but the distinction has real practical importance.

The most important difference between law and equity, other than the right to a jury trial, is that a court of equity can place a person who defies that court's orders in jail until he or she obeys the court. This is about the best technique known—short of the rack or threatened execution—for forcing someone with money to cough up. A court of law, however, cannot employ the same put-him-in-jail technique. If a person recovers a judgment in a contract case or a personal injury case in a court of law, the only method available to collect the judgment is to send a sheriff out to seize any property the defendant owns and sell it. This is a complicated and expensive procedure and, as a result, many judgments that are recovered in courts of law go uncollected.

The distinction between law and equity is critical to a discussion of divorce because it often directly determines how settlement agreements in divorce courts should be handled. A divorce court can do three things with a settlement agreement: (1) it can adopt the agreement and merge it into the divorce decree so that the agreement becomes the order of the court; (2) it can ratify and confirm the agreement but not make the agreement part of the court order and enforceable by the court's put-him-in-jail contempt power; or (3) it can approve the settlement in part as a simple contract enforceable only in a court of law but incorporate other parts of the agreement into the court's own equity order.

When the settlement is merged into the court decree, all the court's contempt powers are available to enforce it. That means the slammer for the solvent but recalcitrant alimony payor if he defaults. Furthermore, since the parties' original agreement has become a decree of a court of equity that has continuing jurisdiction over the parties, the court can at a later time modify the amounts to be paid. When the settlement is only ratified and confirmed, however, it becomes merely a *legal* contract between the parties, so that when one person fails to abide by its terms the only remedy is an action in a court of *law* for a money judgment. That means that the party who needs the money must wait until there is enough at stake to warrant hiring a lawyer and going to court for an expensive trial; it also means that the only way to enforce the judgment is to levy on the defaulter's real and personal property. If the defaulter keeps all his money in a numbered Swiss bank account, it's tough luck. And when the court has only ratified a contract between the parties, it does not have power later to modify the amount to be paid.

Finally, a court can ratify and confirm parts of a settlement and merge others. Typically, a court recites in its order that it "ratifies and confirms" the property settlement agreement; it then establishes the agreed-to amounts of alimony and child support as judicially decreed awards. The obvious pitfall is that, although the dollar amounts in the initial order usually correspond to what the parties agreed to in their settlement, incorporating the agreement into a traditional domestic court order, rather than merely having the settlement contract of the parties "confirmed" by the court, makes both alimony and child support subject to future judicial modification.

There are hundreds of appellate court cases each year on this subject. Typically, they concern the power of a domestic court to change alimony and child support awards after the parties have agreed that future modification will not be allowed. The source of these hotly contested cases is inevitably poor draftsmanship of either the original settlement agreement or the resulting court order. If the parties agree to a sum with the understanding that it will never be modified, the court order must reflect this in some appropriate manner. All contractual deviations from the standard relief that a domestic court is empowered to award must be spelled out with technical precision. If I were representing a husband, I would want to negotiate about whether the contempt remedy would be available in the event of default; and regardless of which party I was representing, I would want to negotiate about whether alimony or periodic payments could be increased or decreased at some future time by the court.

In a similar way, a husband may be willing to continue to pay his former wife periodic payments even if she remarries—something that a divorce court cannot order—in return for her cooperation in maintaining a going business, or for some other concession on her part. But this agreement is very tricky from the wife's side; if a court order does not adequately distinguish between a contractual agreement concerning periodic payments that will continue after remarriage and ordinary, judicially decreed alimony that ends automatically at remarriage, the result is an invitation to endless lawsuits. The husband's argument will be that the court exceeded its legitimate powers in granting alimony after remarriage; the wife will correctly claim that the parties had agreed to that variation. Careful draftsmanship usually prevents lawsuits on such disagreements.

Although the parties can agree to settlement terms that differ from what a court of equity is empowered to decree, those terms will be strictly contractual and enforceable only in a court of law. The parties must understand the consequences of relying on a contract rather than on an order from a court of equity. Enforcing any contract is much more complicated than bringing a contempt-of-court action for nonpayment of alimony. Since in contract cases a person is entitled to a jury trial on many issues—and given the fact that most courts are clogged—it can take as long as four years even to get to trial. Jury trials require juries, courtrooms, supporting court staff, and substantial state expense. For all these reasons contract actions take much longer to be heard than contempt-of-court actions, which can be heard by a judge alone in his or her chambers. Although there is no logical reason why a contract action could not be handled as quickly as a contempt-of-court proceeding, the fact is that the procedure in law courts encourages delay. In New York City, for example, where it takes four to five years to schedule a jury trial, there is a strong incentive to trade away many rights that may have accrued under a contract in return for not having to go to court to secure enforcement.

Furthermore, the rules concerning attorneys' fees differ in lawsuits and in equity proceedings. When a woman sues in a court of law on a contract (unless, as in some states, the contract specifically provides for attorneys' fees for the winning side), she must pay her attorneys' fees. In a contempt-of-court action in a court of equity for failure to pay alimony or support, the court can order the defaulting man to pay the woman's attorney's fees. Consequently, it is worth bargaining about such things as whether the settlement agreement will be "merged" in the court's order or will merely be "ratified and confirmed" by the court.

In West Virginia our supreme court abhors procedural technicalities. We have attempted to eliminate magic-formula terms like "merge" and "ratify and confirm." We allow the parties to express in their divorce settlement contract whatever it is to which they agree: they may specifically provide that the contract is to be enforced by contempt of court; they may agree that the amounts set forth in the contract will never be increased or decreased; they may leave the question of future modification open for the court. But even in a jurisdiction where every effort has been made to eliminate magic-formula words, lawyers who know about the underlying issues in a divorce settlement are needed to draft the agreement and to prepare an appropriate court order for submission to the judge.[2]

My examples concerning drafting divorce decrees are not exhaustive; nor do they represent the problems of any particular locality. More to the point, however, I should reiterate that my examples are not designed to show a person how to be his or her own lawyer but, rather, to show why do-it-yourself lawyering, except in the simplest divorce, is potentially disastrous.

O‍LD lawyers are fond of pointing out that a bad settlement is better than a good lawsuit, but the truth becomes self-evident only when a person understands what a lawsuit entails. Lawsuits are an expensive and chancy business at best. Going to court costs money, and there is also the expense of waiting for whatever decree a court is supposed to give us. Furthermore, courts are unpredictable; every

2. Usually judges do not draft their own court orders. The procedure almost everywhere is for the lawyer who has prevailed in a matter before the court to draft an appropriate court order that must then either be approved by the other side or submitted to the judge with an opportunity for the other side to voice his or her objections. Judges often modify court orders if they have been unskillfully drafted, but the primary responsibility for getting a well-drafted court order that appropriately handles the issues is on the litigants. A good judge may be helpful to an inexperienced lawyer, but an experienced lawyer will be even more helpful to a mediocre or inexperienced judge.

trial lawyer has turned down settlement offers that he or she thought were too low only to go to court and lose everything.

When deciding whether to settle a domestic case or take it to a judge, several questions must be considered: (1) How expensive will it be to go to court? (2) How long will it take to get a judgment, and what will delay itself cost in terms of lawyers' fees, lost income, loss of the use of property, insecurity for children, and so on? (3) What are the chances that the terms of a court decision will be substantially more favorable than the terms of a settlement? (4) What is the likelihood that a voluntary settlement will be honored to a greater extent than a compulsory court judgment after a knock-down fight? A person with anything at all at stake would be foolish to attempt to weigh these matters without the advice of a well-trained lawyer who knows the judges and the law of the area where the case would be tried.

The element of chance in all lawsuits, both criminal and civil, is a result in part of the fact that law involves three distinct and often contradictory elements: substantive rules, the concrete application of those rules, and the procedure through which the rules are translated into some type of court sanction. Before a person can evaluate the quality of his or her lawsuit, he or she must be informed about all the law's substantive principles as well as its technical procedural rules. In most states, for example, if a husband or wife is aware of the other's adultery and still has sexual intercourse with the adulterer, all adultery up to that point is forgiven and cannot be used in evidence to establish fault. This is known as the doctrine of "condonation," and it applies even in circumstances other than adultery (e.g., wife beating). There is not a great deal of sense to that rule today—it is left over from the old consensus when divorce was frowned upon—but it is, nonetheless, alive and well. Furthermore, ignorance of it can lead a litigant to behave in such a way as utterly to destroy his or her lawsuit.

In divorce cases the procedural rules are often at odds with the substantive rules. One example of this situation is that adultery is usually considered the most serious fault-based ground for divorce. However, in many places adultery cannot be proved by testimony of one of the participants in the act. We would think the easiest way to prove adultery would be to call the offending party to the witness stand, place him or her under oath, and ask directly whether he or she had committed adultery—and, if the adulterer's lover were known, to call the lover also as a witness. Yet, because years ago when divorce was frowned upon the courts wanted to discourage collusive divorces, and also because adultery is a low-level crime and asking participants to confess to it in a civil case may raise constitutional questions about forced self-incrimination, the legislatures and the courts created the artificial rule that adultery must be proved by evidence other than by confession of the offending participant(s). That means that husbands and wives must be followed, that hotel or motel records and similar incriminating evidence must be obtained, and that independent witnesses must be found who will testify that they observed the parties under incriminating circumstances. It is hard to prove adultery against a man who commits it with his secretary in the confines of his private office. The wife knows as sure as God made little green apples that he is an adulterer, but she cannot prove it according to the rules of the court.

In order for a litigant to be successful in court, he or she must succeed in each of the three broad areas of substantive rules, concrete application of those rules, and procedural correctness. The litigant must find some general rule covering his or her situation that permits him or her to recover a judgment; the litigant must characterize the facts of his or her case so that his or her situation fits the general rule; and the litigant must accomplish the task of abstracting the facts and fitting them to the general rule in whatever artificial way the court demands. It is insufficient for the litigant to be able to "prove" his or her case by presenting mountains of unrefuted hearsay that any reasonable person would accept or by calling witnesses whom the law refuses to allow to testify. If the artificial rules of evidence that proscribe hearsay and disallow testimony from participants in adultery are not adhered to, the litigant loses his or her case. There is often a lack of harmony among the three integral parts of the law: a litigant can succeed in two of the parts yet fail in the third and lose.

It is difficult if not impossible to predict which of these three aspects of law a judge will find most compelling. If, for example, a case is generally well proved but some piece of hearsay has found its way into the trial, the appellate court can either reverse the judgment or conclude that the offending hearsay was "harmless error" and affirm the judgment. When an appellate court denominates some mistake or other "harmless," that means merely that the result would not conceivably have been different if the error had not been committed.

Some judges are particularly impressed with questions of procedural regularity—they demand that every *i* be dotted and every *t* be crossed. Other judges are exclusively concerned with overall justice—they look at a total trial to

see if substantial justice has been done, and if they conclude that it has, they gloss over technical procedural problems. Similarly, there is enormous diversity among trial
judges: some judges demand a great deal of proof of elements like adultery before being persuaded; some judges
interpret substantive rules idiosyncratically, tolerating
more exceptions or defenses. In one court, for example,
the judge may never permit "cruel and inhuman treatment"
or "mental cruelty" to be a successful defense against adultery, whereas in another court in the same city another
judge may routinely excuse adultery if he or she thinks that
one party drove the other to another's bed.

CONSIDERATIONS such as these militate in favor of hiring a
lawyer. But not all lawyers are qualified to handle divorce
cases. Additionally, some lawyers do one thing in domestic
law well but do others poorly. For example, eager young
lawyers can be very good at collecting support or getting a
divorce for people with little property and few problems.
As a general rule, however, they are less well suited to
drafting settlement agreements and negotiating complicated
property agreements because they have not had sufficient
experience in day-to-day business, income tax law, and
litigation.

Law increasingly is becoming a profession of specialists. The entire body of law is so complicated that there is
little alternative to concentration in specific fields for even
the best-trained and highest-paid lawyers. Some of my own
law school classmates who are now earning $150,000 a year
as practicing lawyers have no more idea about how to try a
divorce case or draft a divorce settlement than about how
to build an atomic bomb; their expertise lies elsewhere.

Legal advice comes in two forms: advice that is free and advice that you pay for. Free advice is tough to beat when it comes from a knowledgeable practicing lawyer. But free advice must be divided into two subcategories: reliable free advice and unreliable free advice. By the same token, these subcategories apply to advice for which you pay dearly.

The best lawyer to handle a divorce is one who specializes to some extent in contested divorce matters and has all the tricky procedural rules firmly committed to memory. When I was practicing small-town divorce law, I was certainly no expert. As I look back on my experience today, I am amazed that apparently I never did anyone any serious damage. Yet during those years I ran into many lawyers on the other side who were even less competent than I was. The bad divorce lawyers fall into four broad profiles.

First is the lawyer who is afraid to go to court. The layperson may think that all lawyers like to go to court, but in fact the opposite is true. Going to court involves a lot of work—witnesses must be summoned, court dates must be obtained, trial court briefs must be written for the judge, and whole days must be blocked out for sitting around waiting for one's turn. Court hearings also involve advocacy skills that many lawyers fear they lack, and consequently many lawyers are notorious cowards about going to court. Although their clients are ignorant of their reputations, other lawyers know all about them. When a client has a lawyer who wants to avoid a court appearance, the lawyer for the other side will demand—and usually receive—extortionate terms in return for an out-of-court settlement.

Second, there are the lawyers who don't care a hoot about their clients. They are in practice for the money, and they treat their clients as meat on the way to dressing and processing. Typically these lawyers live from hand to mouth, and once they receive their fee in advance, they resent the work they must perform to process the client's case. The telltale signs of these lawyers are an overeagerness about payment in advance and an unlisted home telephone number.

Third, there are the kind, gentle, fatherly incompetents. Some lawyers are the salt of the earth—persons of the highest character and most generous natures—but they are dullards when it comes to law. Yet their genuine human qualities, their concern and sympathy, plus their availability (because they have little other work) make them highly attractive. For routine matters these lawyers are wonderful, but if you are in big trouble, they should be avoided.

Finally, there is the innately vicious, mindless litigator. Although the lawyer who is either too lazy or too fearful to go to court presents a problem, the lawyer who wants to litigate everything, who thinks that his or her courtroom skills are so wonderful that he or she will get everything once he or she begins to slug it out, is an even more serious problem. I have seen divorces that, if both lawyers had encouraged good-faith negotiations, could have been settled amicably. But the process was converted into a nightmare by lawyers who didn't know how to settle. Often the professional litigator's idea of bargaining is to demand the whole loaf and then go immediately to court if he or she doesn't get it. This technique may work if there is a cowardly lawyer on the other side, but if the other lawyer is competent it is likely to cost you money while simultaneously painting you into a corner.

Handling a divorce case involves in part the textbook science of law, but it also involves the arts of conciliation and mediation that are instructed by a healthy understanding of human nature. In my experience, clients are unwilling to search out and pay for respected, experienced lawyers when they are seeking a settlement; but this is exactly the wrong approach. When the parties are contemplating a settlement, they need even better advice than when they are planning to go to court. No matter how incompetent a courtroom lawyer is, if the judge is any good at all he or she will attempt to protect everyone's interests. In a settlement, the parties must rely exclusively on their own knowledge of their rights and on their lawyers' skill at negotiation and draftsmanship. The decisive element that determines success in negotiation is a lawyer's firm grasp of the likely result if the case actually goes to court.

One of the greatest dangers of lawyers with a litigating mentality is that they focus exclusively on their client's legal entitlements—the amount of court-ordered alimony, child support, or divided property—without regard to how the other party will respond to an unlivable court order. As I have reiterated throughout this book, receiving a court judgment and enforcing it are two entirely different matters. A settlement that does not work for both parties will not work for either.

When I was in Vietnam, my unit of mixed military and civilian advisors had a superb civilian doctor from California. He had been a successful private physician, but had signed on for service in Vietnam because his wife had gotten a whopping divorce court judgment against him. Rather than pay, he volunteered to serve in Vietnam with the Agency for International Development, and when I left Southeast Asia he was fully resolved to spend the rest of his life banging around the world in remote backwaters so that his wife would never be able to collect a nickel.

Both my doctor friend and his wife could have profited from working out a mutually acceptable settlement. Certainly the doctor would have preferred southern California to Vietnam—at least in the long run—and his wife would have been better off with an award of less money that she received than with an award of more money that she would never see.

It is important in a divorce case to select a lawyer who combines the courage of a litigator with the common sense of a minister. The lawyer must come to some quick conclusions about whether offering reasonable settlement terms will lead to a reasonable response by way of voluntary compliance by the other party. If it appears from a quick evaluation of the adverse party that any order will be resisted, whether it is the product of a settlement or a court battle, nothing is lost by going for broke and trying to get the most favorable agreement or court decree. If, on the other hand, compromise in the area of child custody, support, visitation rights, the allocation of tax burdens, or property division will lead to voluntary and good-faith compliance with the agreement, then over the next twenty years compromise will have gained a great deal more than hardball bargaining or a courtroom showdown.

As I have explained, many areas of disagreement in a divorce can be handled only by a settlement—court-contrived solutions just aren't satisfactory from anyone's point of view. The design of workable plans requires imaginative lawyers. For example, in Chapter 2 I suggested the lump-sum settlement as a way of providing reliable financial support for the wife while at the same time giving the husband a definite obligation that would never change for the worse. Yet a court cannot order such an arrangement; a court cannot tell a husband to borrow $50,000 to settle for all time his obligations.

Furthermore, it is almost impossible for courts to make efficient arrangements to apportion pension rights and interests in going businesses. Ownership interests in businesses are often like ownership interests in a table. If we cut a table in half, we don't emerge with two small tables; we emerge with two useless pieces of junk. At least theoretically a court ought to be able to engineer arrangements that permit both parties to exploit their joint assets, but in practice court-imposed schemes for this purpose usually end up as invitations to a lifetime of litigation, which then makes the lawyers at least one-third beneficiaries in whatever fruits the assets produce.

It is easy for a court to divide stock in large, publicly held corporations. Everyone knows that these stocks will pay reasonable dividends every quarter, and shares in such companies can be sold easily and quickly. Stock in smaller, publicly held corporations can also be divided with some assurance that reasonable dividends will be paid. But stock in a small, closely held corporation has very little value to a minority stockholder if the majority stockholder or stockholders decide to freeze the minority stockholder out. When I was in law school, we memorized the axiom, "Never take a minority position in a small corporation." We all knew the theoretical remedies available to minority stockholders who were being taken to the cleaners. We also knew just how expensive, chancy, and time-consuming it is to use these remedies. Prevention is a lot better than cure.

In a small, going business it is difficult to determine how much profit is attributable to invested capital and how much to the owners' labor. Most small businesses, such as gas stations, clothing stores, and family farms, yield their owners a lower return for hours worked than those owners could earn by taking comparable hourly or salaried jobs with large companies. Many people who own small businesses essentially pay for the privilege of working for themselves.

In fact, in most small corporations everything the corporation earns is paid out in salaries to the owners of the stock: family-owned corporations seldom show a profit because doing so would result in unnecessary double taxation. When a corporation makes a profit, it must pay a corporation income tax, and when the profits are passed on to owners, they must pay income tax on the same money. It is sufficiently difficult to allocate returns to labor and returns to capital in small corporations that even the Internal Revenue Service makes no serious effort to collect the taxes that might be owed. The IRS will generally accept tax returns that show corporations going on for years without making a penny of profit.

A domestic court cannot compel a husband or wife to borrow money against his or her stock in a small business to provide a lump-sum settlement. All the court can do is split the stock or award alimony based on the expected return on investment in the business. If the court splits the stock, who is to say that a dividend will ever be paid to the minority stockholder? The same applies to a pension. If the pension is vested and money is deposited with a pension trustee to fund the pension, the beneficiary may be able to withdraw the money. If the beneficiary can withdraw money, the court can split the pension assets. If, however, the money cannot be withdrawn—something that is routine in government pensions at all levels—all the court can do is give other property to offset the value of the pension or, if there is no other property, allow the proceeds from the pension to be tapped at a later time. In my estimation, none of these options is as advantageous to either party as some sort of clean, lump-sum settlement—but that usually requires willingness to use borrowing power, something a court cannot require.

It is a simple rule of legal practice that the more complicated a court's order, the more difficult it is to enforce. When one person has cash in hand and another person has an arguable legal right to that cash, the person with the cash has the advantage. At the simplest level, as I explained in Chapter 4, it is much more expensive to prosecute a lawsuit than it is to defend one, and the transactional costs of prosecution often preclude any prosecution.

This is a brief sketch of some of the most vexatious common problems. A good, livable divorce settlement for a middle-class, middle-aged couple requires lawyers, ones who have experience, imagination, and good human relations skills. For not only must they figure out a bargain that is advantageous to both clients, but they must also be able to explain it to their clients in such a way as to elicit willing acquiescence. Lawyers with these skills can not only work good deals; they can also eliminate or reduce future litigation, make things easier for children and relatives, and keep the costs of getting a divorce to a minimum. Such lawyers are a good investment.

Some jurisdictions permit lawyers to represent *both* parties in a divorce proceeding. The reason is economic— one lawyer is about half as expensive as two. This type of arrangement is obviously risky. It works if there are no children, little property, and no alimony—and if both parties have almost no disagreements. Couples with that degree of mutual concern and understanding usually don't get divorced.

There is no getting around the fact that divorce is adversarial. In any given family, the hours that children spend with their parents, the future earning capacities of the husband and wife, and all the accumulated property constitute a pie of a given size. Divorce splits up that pie, and a larger slice for one person necessarily means a smaller slice for the other. It is impossible for one lawyer simultaneously to advise each party to a divorce to demand a bigger slice of the pie.

A lawyer who represents both parties to a divorce will usually have been a friend of both parties or the lawyer for one of them. If the lawyer is a family friend, he or she will be placed in the position of a mediator. The lawyer will advise both parties what arrangement would be fair to them but will probably not advise both parties what position they could take in a go-for-broke courtroom battle. Such a mediator takes some crucial decisions away from the litigants. The lawyer, not the parties, decides on the settlement in much the same way that a judge would. Although this process has its charm—not the least of which is low-level, low-pressure mediation—usually neither party is informed of all available options. Litigants may be willing to relinquish certain legal rights out of a sense of fairness to their spouses. They should not, however, relinquish rights they don't even know they have.

If the lawyer representing both parties was initially the lawyer for one party alone, a serious problem arises. Inevitably the lawyer will favor his or her own client, and although the lawyer will be reluctant to allow an outrageously one-sided agreement to be entered into, nonetheless, the agreement will probably favor the lawyer's initial client.

Regardless of whether we are talking about do-it-your-self lawyering, hiring one lawyer for both parties, or finding a lawyer who is cheap and available, we reach the same conclusion: a person's caution in the divorce process should be a direct function of what is at stake. Two twenty-three-year-olds—he a factory worker and she a secretary —have very little to lose from being their own divorce lawyers. They have no property that is difficult to divide, and it is unlikely that a court would award alimony to such a young woman. But if this couple has children, there are enough potential problems that both parties need some good professional advice.

Older couples need better advice. For example, the Social Security Administration has an arbitrary rule concerning wives' entitlements to Social Security. If a woman has been married to a man for ten years or longer, she is entitled to a Social Security pension based on his earnings. However, if she has been married less than ten years, she must take under her own entitlement; if she has not worked at a high wage, her entitlement may be negligible. It would be silly for a woman to get a divorce after nine and a half years of marriage when waiting another six months would vest Social Security retirement benefits that neither party pays for directly.

There is one final thing that an experienced lawyer can do for a person: a lawyer can help a person decide whether a divorce is really in his or her best interests. When an individual initially concludes that divorce is the way to go, the focus of attention is usually on the emotional rather than on the economic aspects of married life. Good divorce lawyers can explain the economic consequences of divorce so that a person can make a more informed judgment concerning the advantages and disadvantages of taking that course of action.

Reading general books like this one on divorce may give a person some insight into what divorce is all about, but most divorce books are written for national audiences and therefore talk in general terms. Each state's divorce laws have their own eccentricities, and every person's economic and emotional life is unique. Priests, doctors, and marriage counselors may be good advisors concerning the general implications of divorce, but a lawyer can make divorce's economic consequences come into focus. In Indiana, for instance, there is no alimony. When a woman gets divorced there, regardless of her age, the length of the marriage, or her earning potential, she gets her share of the family's assets and nothing more. How, therefore, a woman residing in Indiana—or a man, for that matter—views the desirability of divorce will be entirely different from the views of the same person living in Illinois. Only an Indiana lawyer can explain the peculiarities of that state's law and give specific advice to an Indiana client.

If a person has anything whatsoever at stake in a divorce—children, property, a going business or pension rights, an income-earning potential, or years of accumulated service as a homemaker—$1,000 of good legal advice is cheap. Choose a lawyer who specializes in divorce and who will go to court when necessary but is smart enough to understand the value of conciliation, mediation, and negotiation. The problem for most people is determining which lawyer fits this profile. In the final analysis, seeking out the best advice costs more time than money. But a few hours of consultation with friends and acquaintances concerning lawyers they know will usually yield the right person.

6

Marriage Contracts, Living Together, and Palimony

In 1975 I wrote a magazine article about marriage contracts. The article led to an invitation to discuss marriage contracts on ABC's "Good Morning America" and caused me some notoriety as a proponent of marriage contracts at the high point of America's flirtation with alternative lifestyles. Four years later, at the age of thirty-eight, I got married. Among my friends there was amused curiosity concerning what my own marriage contract looked like.

The truth is that I never drafted a contract for my own marriage. This was not just another instance—like the lawyer who dies without a will or the doctor who smokes two packs of cigarettes a day—where a professional was too lazy or too weak-willed to take his own advice. Although I was intimately familiar with marriage contracts and, in fact, had a drawer full of model forms that had been sent to me by lawyers from around the country, I found that West Virginia's laws surrounding marriage were as close to what my wife and I contemplated in our relationship as anything we could draft ourselves.

Everyone who gets married becomes a party to a complex marriage contract. This fact is often obscured by the deceptive brevity of the marriage ceremony. Civil ceremonies are usually less than three hundred words, religious ceremonies not much longer. Yet the standard ceremony, or any other ceremony of the parties' creation, binds people to a contract so complex that it defies reduction to a written document.

For example, the state-imposed marriage contract sets forth a scheme for distributing a married person's property when he or she dies. Although a person can disinherit his or her children, he or she cannot disinherit a spouse. Almost everywhere a surviving spouse is entitled to at least a third of the mate's property. In addition, most states give a surviving spouse the right to live in the family home for the rest of his or her life.

Both husband and wife must sign deeds transferring any real property owned by them individually. This is because each spouse is entitled to a one-third life interest in all real property owned by the other spouse during the marriage. Therefore, when a person gets married, he or she automatically receives a valuable interest in all real estate owned by his or her spouse. This interest in real estate is called "dower," and it is a holdover from the days when people farmed and a family's wealth consisted of land. Dower was created and still persists in the law to assure that valuable property, (e.g., a house or a farm), is not sold by one spouse for cash that can then be squandered without the other spouse's consent. In all but two states—Mississippi and Virginia—the marriage contract implies that assets acquired through joint efforts during the marriage will be equitably divided (or, in community-property states, split fifty-fifty) on the dissolution of the marriage.

Few people who walk down the aisle for the first time to repeat a little mumbo-jumbo about "love, honor and cherish" and "till death us do part" have given much thought to the contractual side of marriage. Even those who do understand that marriage imposes legal and ethical as well as emotional obligations are usually aware of only the broadest outlines of the terms of the contract to which they are assenting. This is not surprising; most people routinely sign leases and contracts that they haven't read.

In small business, as in marriage, we do business with our friends and don't expect them to cheat us or take undue advantage of us. In both undertakings, methodically attempting to get everything understood in advance and reduced to writing kills good deals more often than it saves us from bad ones. As in business, although people may not entirely understand the small-print terms of their marriages, they know the rough outline of the deal well enough to decide whether they want to participate.

PEOPLE who have lived with someone of the opposite sex on a long-term basis without getting married have often concluded that they do not like the deal. If they expressed their reservations in business terms, they would say that too much money is riding on too little security. Up until about the mid-1960s, a decision not to get married implied that one would have to live alone or with a roommate of the same sex. Society imposed sanctions upon people of opposite sex who wanted to live together out of wedlock.

Landlords often evicted unmarried persons living together; employers fired them; and occasionally an irate father beat the hell out of them.

All that has changed. Living together is beginning to compete with marriage as a long-term way of life for all social classes and all age groups. In 1970, 523,000 heterosexual unmarried couples lived together. By 1980 the number had skyrocketed to 1,560,000, an increase of roughly 200 percent.

People choose to live together without benefit of wedlock for a variety of reasons. Some may view marriage as an institution that has outlived its social usefulness. Others may be forced into such an arrangement either because dissolving a prior marriage is too complicated or expensive or, as among many older people, because they lose legal entitlements that flow to them as single individuals. The largest number of these couples, however, are young people who want a trial period of living together before making a formal and lasting commitment. Frequently the decision not to marry is one-sided on the part of the person in the superior financial position. He or she may enjoy the companionship of the other person and benefit from the division of labor inherent in joint households but still be unwilling to expose himself or herself to the risk to property that marriage entails.

The existence of an attractive and acceptable alternative lifestyle is to some a cause for celebration. The wholesale rejection of marriage, however, throws a monkey wrench into the complicated social machinery that is designed to give people security against illness, old age, and poverty—particularly the poverty of single parenthood. This society is designed for married couples, and people who do not undertake the obligations of marriage, for whatever reason, find that they do not qualify for a host of public and private benefits.

Divorce laws try to protect women and children to some extent against the poverty that the dissolution of a joint household entails, but these laws are only a small part of the overall protective package. Social Security, employer pension and health benefits, inheritance rights, and rights in real property are all tied to marital relationships. The reason for this has less to do with what was once inscribed on stone tablets than with what is currently entered on actuarial tables.

Whatever its moral import, marriage, as I explained in Chapter 1, offers enormous economies of scale. From an actuarial point of view, both private and government social welfare programs assume these economies of scale in calculating the value of benefits. In other words, if it can be assumed that men and women usually live together in joint households, it costs us all less to provide basic economic security for the elderly, the disabled, and dependent children. If a majority of Americans decide that marriage is obsolete, we will need to redesign our entire social insurance apparatus; and if this occurs the costs will more than double. Social Security taxes, for example, would take 32 percent of the current wage fund instead of the current 16 percent.

A sociology student might ask why cohabiting couples cannot be given the benefits of social programs designed for married couples. The answer involves considerations that go beyond the increased costs of benefits resulting from lost economies of scale. The first consideration is that under the traditional marriage laws a person can be married to only one person at a time. The Social Security Administration knows that if I am a dues-paying member of its program it will need to pay benefits only to my wife and, more to the point, to only one wife. If two or more persons claim benefits as my wife, the Social Security Administration knows that a state court will determine which claim should be honored. In terms of how many people can claim retirement benefits under my account number, the limited options allow for actuarial soundness: I can either have one wife or no wife. If, on the other hand, a person can have one cohabiting partner, why not two or three? There are no available or readily imaginable criteria for deciding which partner gets the benefits.

An employer can provide a pension for a worker and his or her spouse, but he must know in advance how many claimants will qualify for benefits. If cohabiting partners come forward to claim benefits, the actuaries will go berserk because the cost of these claims has not been budgeted into the system, nor has the cost of litigation to determine who is entitled to the benefits if entitlement is limited to the one cohabiting mate who looks most like a traditional wife or husband. Similar problems arise with respect to children. Legitimate children can be provided for under health and survivors' insurance programs. If, however, anyone with a job can give any child of his or her choosing the right to use his or her health card, insurance rates would skyrocket.

The critic can say that a system that ties economic benefits to observance of traditional social mores is unfair. The answer, I am afraid, is that our system of government and employer benefits is unfair in that it does not treat everyone equally. For example, it retains a bias from yesteryear that favors married households where only one person works. Thus, married people who both work are penalized a little by the tax system; retired couples who both work at high-paying jobs will get a lower return for their contributions to Social Security than will couples who have only one worker; and employers—particularly government employers—deduct the same amount in retirement contributions from both single and married employees, notwithstanding the fact that the cost of a married worker's pension may be a third again as expensive as a single worker's pension, since usually the surviving spouse of a married worker is also entitled to benefits.

These inequities, however, are more than counterbalanced by the beneficent purposes and effects of entitlement systems that attempt to redistribute wealth to those in need when they are the victims of bad luck. Social Security's "preference" for the single-worker family does not point toward a pernicious conspiracy to keep women at home. It reflects a recognition of the economic reality that a family with only one steady source of income is less likely to be able to build its own safety net against poverty and/or old age.

The old way of doing things, which held that people of opposite sex who wanted to enjoy the emotional and economic benefits of a joint household had to sign onto the marriage rolls, had more going for it than old-fashioned sexual morality. If marriage does nothing else, it regularizes who can qualify for property division, inheritance, private and public pensions, and survivors' benefits. Under the marriage system, when a joint household splits up a formal divorce is required, and a court settles all existing rights to property, insurance benefits, and pensions. When people live together and then split up, there is no similar formal and reliable regulation of who gets what.[1] The result is that nobody knows what, if anything, he or she is entitled to receive.

The Victorian morality that dominated England and America in the latter half of the nineteenth and the first half of the twentieth centuries was an aberration. Henry Fielding gives us far more insight into the norms of social and sexual affairs than does Anthony Trollope.[2] Contrary to popular belief, living together without marriage is a very old custom. As early as 1809 the State of New York recognized the "marriage of couples who, without benefit of clergy, lived together and acted as husband and wife." Thirteen states continue to recognize common-law marriages, although the standard for proving such relationships has stiffened.

In light of the ever-growing number of unmarried, co-

1. The Social Security laws regarding both pension and survivors' benefits attempt to be practical about these matters. For example, a spouse's pension rights vest after ten years of marriage, so that a divorced spouse who has never worked, or worked at low-paying jobs, can still claim under the account of her or his former spouse. Furthermore, Social Security recognizes the doctrine of "equitable adoption" under which if a family breadwinner dies leaving minor children that he or she has been raising destitute—even if they were never formally adopted—Social Security will pay survivors' benefits to the children just as if they had lost their father or mother. Usually, however, this rule is applied in cases where children are being raised by their grandparents.

2. Certainly the history of modern England did not begin on a morally auspicious note. At the Battle of Hastings in 1066, both antagonists—William the Conqueror and Harold Godwin the Saxon—were either the product of an illicit cohabitation or a party to one. William, who was known affectionately as "the Bastard," was the product of a long-term, unsanctified relationship between his father, Duke Robert of Normandy, and Arlette of Falaise. Harold, for his part, lived almost his entire adult life in an unsanctified, "hand-fast" union with Edith Swan-neck. He officially married Aldgyth, of the politically powerful Northumbrian house of Leofric, for reasons of state only after becoming king in 1066.

habiting couples, the law must decide how it will treat these people. In this regard, a revitalization of the older doctrines concerning "common-law marriages" would be useful in some cases, but the application would be limited. All unmarried couples are not the same. For example, couples who live together for a semester in a college dormitory or an apartment do not present a perplexing legal or social problem. That kind of arrangement has little in common with anything resembling marriage. The law everywhere is that whoever has the room or apartment in his or her name can pretty well say sayonara to his or her roommate without any legal inconvenience.

Some couples have lived together for many years, pooling their financial resources and rearing the children of their union. These couples have all the attributes of married people. In the states that recognize common-law marriage these long-term partners would receive the entitlements of a married couple if neither was married to another. In the states that do not explicitly recognize common-law marriages, the courts would probably attempt to give both partners the benefits of marital status by cutting and bending traditional contract law.

Unfortunately, most of the cases that actually come to court are less clear-cut. They are likely to involve parties who had, or at least claim to have had, different expectations regarding the permanence of their relationship. Just as married couples don't analyze their daily actions with respect to how they will be viewed by a divorce court, people living together don't know how a court will interpret their actions. Does the fact that a car was bought with pooled funds at a time when neither party could afford one individually point toward a relationship akin to marriage?

Do separate checking accounts maintained to assure independent credit ratings mean that there were no joint economic interests? The legal answers to those questions have not yet been crafted, and when courts are on novel ground, the parties who come to them seeking solutions are on shaky ground too.

The 1979 case that declared Lee Marvin's live-in female companion entitled to "palimony" generated national attention as a "trend-setting" case. In fact, it was a unique situation that does not resemble real life as most of us know it. Lee Marvin has a lot of money, so a recovery that takes only a small percentage of his total assets makes a long and expensive lawsuit appear worthwhile.[3] Since few people cohabit with millionaires, very few cohabiting people will find competent, energetic lawyers who are willing to take their speculative, difficult cases for palimony without the payment of a big up-front fee.

Most long-term cohabitants choose the same people to live with as they would have married—clerical workers, salespersons, factory workers. These people have nothing in common with Lee Marvin. They are in debt, and they do not have any valuable property to divide. Their most valuable assets are usually pension rights and government entitlements like Social Security, which are extremely difficult for a cohabiting partner to tap.

Moreover, although five states have followed the *Marvin* decision and explicitly upheld mutual property rights

3. In the end, the trial court awarded only $104,000 to Michelle Marvin, less than 10 percent of the $1.8 million she had sought. Most estimates place her attorney's (Marvin Mitchelson) total fee at five times the amount recovered. The moral of the story is that even when the pocket is deep attorneys take a risk in handling such speculative cases, and therefore live-ins should not expect competent counsel to line up anxiously awaiting their business.

for unmarried couples on the basis of an explicit or implicit contractual agreement to joint ownership, the law does not treat unmarried couples at all like married couples. Getting a property division or palimony award for an unmarried partner is an uphill battle everywhere because courts have not abandoned the "illegal consideration" doctrine. Most states still make fornication a misdemeanor criminal offense, and almost all states make adultery a misdemeanor criminal offense. Although prosecutions for fornication or adultery are as rare as undergraduates who read *Paradise Lost* in their spare time, when illicit sexual relations form the consideration for a joint living arrangement—in other words, if a man agrees to support a woman in return for her sleeping with him—the contract is void as against public policy. Judges are about as modern as the rest of us, however, and courts understand that what may start as only a passionate sexual attachment can mature into the kind of mutual living arrangement that is associated with marriage. In such a circumstance, courts try to sever that part of the contract centering on sex and uphold the remaining part. This is an artificial exercise, but it continues to pay lip service to our traditions that disfavor meretricious relationships.

Because in the last ten years there has been a 200 percent increase in the number of couples cohabiting out of wedlock, many more cases involving the dissolution of nonmarried households will hit the courts in the next several years. The highest courts of some states will inevitably take a very hard, moralistic line. This is what Georgia did in 1977 in *Rehak* v. *Mathis,* where the state's high court barred recovery by a woman who for eighteen years cooked, cleaned, and cared for a man; contributed money for the purchase of a home; and made several mortgage payments. When the man died the woman went to court to get her fair share of his estate, but the Georgia court held that the oral express agreement by a married man to make a woman the irrevocable beneficiary of his life insurance policy in return for her society and companionship (read "sex") is void because it is against public policy.

Other, less fundamentalist courts are likely to apply ad hoc, and for that reason unpredictable, principles of fairness case by case without undertaking a frontal assault on traditional morality. That is what New York did in *McCall v. Frampton*. A lower court had dismissed a woman's suit as violating public policy because she had been married to another man when she began her six-year cohabitation with Frampton. The plaintiff alleged that she was heavily involved with Frampton's work and that an oral agreement existed between them to share the profits of his business. Although the trial court held that the agreement was void because the relationship was adulterous, a Class B misdemeanor in New York, the appellate court reversed and reinstated two of her claims, the most important being her claim for money under a five-year contract of partnership with Frampton. The appellate court held that there is no automatic forfeiture of rights under a lawful business agreement just because the partners also decide to live together.

THERE are three broad classes of cases involving cohabiting persons. The first class contains cases like *Frampton* where the cohabiting persons have a common interest in an economic enterprise. Typically, all the assets of the enterprise are in the man's name, and the woman is asking for a division of property she helped to acquire. At one extreme, this type of case is no more difficult than an ordinary lawsuit between business partners; if both people have been actively engaged in the management of the enterprise, the fact that they have had a sexual relationship is easily factored out of consideration. The more likely situation, however, is that the woman helped the man the way an employee would but received her compensation in the form of support as a traditional wife would. In that circumstance, the case looks more like a regular divorce where a court is required to divide jointly acquired property on some equitable basis. Unless the woman can prove a contractual agreement in a case like that, it is unlikely that she will recover anything.

The second class of cases involves palimony—actions by cohabiting members of the opposite sex for continuing support when a long-term relationship breaks up. The plaintiff in such a case will usually be a woman who wants both an equitable division of jointly acquired property and continuing court-ordered support. The woman's argument for support will be that her long-term cohabiting relationship should be treated just like a marriage because the economic results, in terms of forgone opportunities, are exactly the same.[4]

4. Cases can certainly be envisaged where the complaining party is a man. Wealthy women who want the long-term companionship of younger men can be as vulnerable to actions of this sort as their male counterparts. Such cases, however, are not worth much discussion here because they are rare.

Far more common are cases involving cohabiting couples of the same sex. In light of the increasing numbers of long-term gay relationships, the fair allocation of jointly acquired property and consideration of rights to continuing support is a serious social and legal issue. Because the contract of marriage is currently reserved for partners of opposite sexes, single-sex couples have little alternative

My belief is that courts would be more sympathetic to a request for the equitable division of property than to a request for continuing support. One reason for this belief is that property division is something courts do all the time in contexts other than divorce. Dividing jointly acquired property does not require the application of principles unique to domestic law. Continuing support, on the other hand, is a remedy associated only with traditional marriage, and allowing that remedy to unmarried persons will ultimately involve a confrontation with the moral principles that still surround marriage.

More important, judges are likely to believe that general notions of equity require some division of jointly held property but that the imposition of continuing support obligations would frustrate the intent of parties who had implicitly rejected that obligation by rejecting traditional marriage. Continuing support is likely to be allowed only in circumstances where the relationship has been so long—say, twenty years—that the courts can hold that there was a de facto marriage and, in effect, resurrect the doctrine of common-law marriage.

The last class of cases involves the death of one of the cohabiting partners and the rights of the other partner to inherit his or her estate. These are very difficult cases, particularly if the deceased was already legally married to

when their relationship breaks up than to petition courts to apply new, creative doctrines of contract law. Because this is a book about divorce—which implies the dissolution of relationships between partners of opposite sex—discussion of the problems of single-sex couples is beyond its scope. Nevertheless, the problems of single-sex couples must eventually be confronted by the courts in both an intelligent and sensitive way, and exclusion of the matter here is merely in deference to the practical consideration that books must be written for one audience at a time.

someone else, even though he or she may not have seen the spouse for twenty years. As I indicated earlier, marriage creates very specific statutory property rights that cannot be manipulated by courts applying equitable principles.[5]

Every state has a statute concerning the distribution of a person's property if he or she dies without a will. Ordinarily, if there is no will a spouse takes half and children take the other half (if there are both a spouse and children). If there are no children, the spouse gets it all. The kicker, however, is that if there is neither official spouse nor legitimate (or, under certain complicated circumstances, illegitimate) children, then parents, siblings, nephews, nieces, and finally cousins take everything under the intestate succession statute in preference to a live-in housemate of even thirty years' duration.[6]

5. Possibly this is a bit of an overstatement. There is nothing in the law so definite that a strong-willed court cannot manipulate it. It would be more accurate to say that courts adhering to the generally accepted doctrine of legislative supremacy in all areas where the legislature has lawmaking discretion under the Constitution will have a hard time defeating a spouse's statutory right to inheritance without looking like lawless and unprofessional buffoons.

6. A good example of this problem involved my own mother, although she was not cohabiting. My mother's father died very young, and her mother pursued a fairly lucrative career. As a result, my mother was reared from about the age of twelve by my grandmother's best friend, whom my mother always called Aunt Mertle. When Aunt Mertle's husband died about 1936, my mother accompanied Aunt Mertle—who had no children—to California. My mother visited with Aunt Mertle in her old age, wrote to her regularly, and generally gave her the emotional support that a child would provide. One day Aunt Mertle died suddenly, leaving no will. She left no property of any financial value, but she did leave property, like her wedding ring, of sentimental value. The State of California took her few possessions, boxed them up, and sent them to her brother, a resident of Canada whom she had not seen, heard from, nor written to for fifty years. Yet he was entitled under the law to all her worldly goods, and if my mother had spent $1,000 in legal fees her chances of getting even the wedding ring would have been vanishingly small.

Inheritance is not always barred for a live-in mate. A court can declare a cohabiting relationship a de facto marriage and then apply the rules of inheritance applicable to marriages to it. The longer the couple had been living together, the better the claimant's chance of making that argument work. Also, if a person does not have a living spouse, and as long as the person is competent and not the victim of "undue influence," he or she can write a will and leave the property to anyone at all—from a live-in housemate to a charity for wayward cats. Courts, however, have often found "undue influence" on the part of the live-in housemates when children are disinherited; and no matter what a will says, a living spouse will always get half or a third of the estate, even if he or she is in prison, a mental hospital, or is permanently comatose and being kept alive on life-support systems.

In all three classes of cases—business partnership, long-term relationships where continuing support is sought, and inheritance—the outcome will be affected by whether the party with the money was already married and to what extent he or she has maintained a continuing relationship with his or her official spouse. If, for example, a man is married, has children, and continues his relationship with his family while at the same time keeping a traditional "mistress," it is unlikely that a court will award the "mistress" property or palimony even if the relationship was a long-standing one.

A woman in such circumstances does not arouse judicial sympathy because she is aware that the man is married and has obligations to his legitimate family. A court's decision would be instructed in part by the fact that any money awarded to the "mistress" will take assets away from that family. An adulterous relationship has less effect on the dissolution of a business partnership, but the person claiming a share of assets not in his or her name would need to prove that he or she contributed significant business-related services pursuant to some explicit agreement to share the profits from the business. Illegitimate children resulting from an adulterous relationship, however, have just as strong a claim on their father's continuing support as do legitimate children. This rule follows from the twin considerations that the children are innocent and that, if the father does not support them, the rest of us will.

The lack of specificity in the discussion so far has probably left the reader's thirst for information about how courts will treat our new living arrangements unquenched. Unfortunately, it is impossible to be definite. Different state courts, composed as they are of different people with different philosophies, will inevitably handle these matters in different ways. Although the law is changing, judges are not writing on a clean slate. As I mentioned earlier, adultery and illicit cohabitation are still low-level crimes in most states, and there are years of accumulated precedent disfavoring these relationships.

Two observations, however, can be made with some certainty. First, a person in a strong financial position can no longer rely on the absence of formal wedding vows to protect his or her property and income if he or she enters into a long-term relationship with an economically weaker party. If a man lulls a woman into a false sense of security for many years, encouraging her to forego other options—either in the form of a career or formal marriage to another—many courts will not allow him to walk away from their joint household with the same lack of legal complications that would attend the conclusion of a weekend romance.

The second observation is that formal marriage protects a woman to an astronomically greater extent than any of the emerging rules on cohabiting couples. With the stroke of a pen, a one-gallused justice of the peace can establish a wife's right to a portion of her husband's estate; her right to elect to take under his Social Security entitlement; her right to an equitable distribution of property acquired during marriage if they split up; and in most places, if the divorce is not her fault, her right to support for life or at least until she is able to support herself.

The woman who chooses to devote years to a wealthy married man is in about the worst position. Even courts that look favorably on the claims of long-term cohabiting partners when both are single are put off by the claims of a "mistress" because the family of a married man have a legitimate ironclad legal claim to whatever money he earns. Many homes probably deserve to be broken, but the law is not subtle about these things, nor can it be. Divorce is the legally accepted way of dissolving a relationship because that process settles once and for all the property rights established by the marriage contract between the divorcing parties.

ONE conclusion that emerges is that marriage is a contractual arrangement with some fairly definite terms and quite a few not-so-definite terms. People may accept some of these terms but not others. A person with property or an income potential to protect may be perfectly happy about marriage's terms concerning the distribution of property at death, entitlements to Social Security and pensions, and the legitimization of any potential children with all that implies concerning their rights to inherit in the event of death without a will. That same person may balk at the thought of some low-level domestic relations judge rearranging his property and income in the event that the marriage doesn't work.

People may also be reluctant to have a judge decide questions of custody, visitation rights, and even educational programs for the children—something that often happens when a couple divorce. It occurred to many people during the 1970s when divorce was becoming as common as long-term marriage that custom-made marriage contracts might eliminate people's exposure to certain of the more terrifying risks of divorce with regard to such matters as alimony, property division, child custody, support, and education. This is what I believed in 1975 when I wrote the magazine article on marriage contracts. It was only after eight more years of experience and of thinking through the problem that I began to realize that marriage contracts have only a limited application. They appear elegantly efficient in theory, but they are woefully inadequate in practice.

Marriage contracts are a time-honored contrivance that have been upheld by courts for centuries. However, until recently they have been used almost exclusively in a specific circumstance—second marriages. The reason for their use in second marriages goes back to the statutes on inheritance. Without a marriage contract, the inheritance rights of children from a first marriage may be jeopardized by a second marriage.

Typically, a husband and wife will get married in their twenties and raise children together. As a result of their joint efforts, substantial property may be accumulated that they want to pass on to their children. If the wife dies first, the husband will be in possession of all the property.[7] If a widower marries a second time without a marriage contract, his second wife will be entitled to one-half or one-third, depending on the state, of his property at his death, which she may then leave to anyone she wishes, including her own children by a previous marriage or collateral relatives. Such an arrangement would be a substantial impediment to second marriages were some device not contrived to protect the rights of children from first marriages. Because the general law regarding the inheritance rights of spouses is set up primarily for people in first marriages, we have always permitted people in second marriages to enter into a contract before (*never* after) marriage waiving statutory rights to inheritance.

The question remains whether persons entering first marriages can similarly alter the state-imposed obligations of marriage on subjects other than inheritance (something about which young people think very little) by writing their own contracts. Can a woman, for example, by prenuptial

7. It used to be that people with large estates would leave only half their estates or $250,000—whichever was greater—to their spouses because that was as much as could pass tax-free. Unless the spouse needed more to live, the remainder was left to children in order to avoid double estate taxation. Since the amendments to the federal estate tax statutes in 1981, however, it is more intelligent to leave only so much of one's estate as is exempt from federal taxation—a graduated amount that goes up every year until 1986 when it will be $600,000—to children, and everything else to the spouse. The reason is that now all money passing to a spouse is tax-free, and so all money saved in taxes can be invested at compound interest. There is no longer a double taxation problem. Of course, tax considerations and personal considerations may not be parallel, and obviously most estates have less than $600,000. Nonetheless, for very large estates the change in the tax statutes has had a major impact on estate planning and how much money remains in the hands of a widow or widower.

contract forever abjure her right to alimony and an equitable division of family property in the event of divorce? Can people regulate in advance awards of custody, terms of child support, and entitlements to alimony by contract?

Most couples entering first marriages don't bother to draft agreements on these subjects. Detailed, prearranged terms of divorce tend to have a chilling effect on the urge to get married and may increase tensions about lost autonomy. Furthermore, most couples could not agree on the terms. Therefore, although the question of the validity of such agreements is interesting in the abstract, very few cases involving prenuptial agreements among couples in first marriages have actually reached the courts.

If, however, people begin to use marriage contracts in contexts other than the traditional one of protecting family property in second marriages, it is unlikely that courts will look on them with favor. Courts are reluctant to enforce one-sided contracts that are the product of unequal bargaining power, and it doesn't take a genius to figure out that the people most likely to use marriage contracts are sophisticated men who want to protect their income and property. There are numerous legal devices that can be used to invalidate unfair contracts in commercial contexts, many of which would be mobilized to invalidate one-sided marriage contracts.

When we borrow money from a bank, we need the money more than the bank needs to make the loan. Similarly, when we buy a car, we need the transportation more than General Motors needs to sell us its two millionth Chevrolet. Furthermore, GM sells cars every day and Chase Manhattan makes loans every hour, so they are unlikely to alter the terms of the deal in an individual case. In such circumstances the party in the stronger bargaining position will inevitably want to stick clauses in the contract that eliminate almost all the rights of the consumer. An example of this in banking contracts is the "confession of judgment" clause under which, when the bank finds the loan in default, it can go to court and get an enforceable judgment without serving the debtor with process or giving him or her a hearing. In automobile contracts the classic example is the contract clause that relieves the manufacturer of any liability for a defective car, so that if a wheel falls off when you are doing fifty-five, you cannot sue the manufacturer for the inevitable injuries.

Courts have held these types of contractual clauses "unconscionable"—they refuse to enforce such clauses because they exceed the bounds of what parties in roughly equal bargaining positions would negotiate for themselves. What makes a clause "unconscionable" is largely a subjective judgment on the part of courts. Almost all contracts are entered into by parties of different bargaining power. In these cases there is always a tension between doctrines that favor freedom of contract and countervailing doctrines that protect the weak or unwary from extortionate terms. Because marriage is an institution that forms the foundation of this society and is already heavily regulated by the courts, when marriage contracts come up for court review any arguments about the desirability of freedom of contract drawn from commercial contexts will probably be unpersuasive. A person who relies on a one-sided marriage contract is likely to be treated very roughly by the courts.

In addition to the problem of unequal bargaining power, one-sided marriage contracts may be considered violations of public policy. The argument is simply that society is better off if married couples stay married. Courts will not enforce contracts that facilitate divorce, a socially undesirable result. It is true that divorce is a common practice, but it need not follow that courts will look favorably on mechanisms that make it even more prevalent.

One further general observation about contract law is in order: contracts are strongest and most enforceable when the parties have correctly foreseen potential problems. A court is more likely to enforce a contract in its own explicit terms if all the assumptions on which the contract was predicated continue to be valid. If a company agrees to deliver so many barrels of oil on a particular date but war breaks out closing off the Persian Gulf, a court is likely to release the oil company from its obligation to deliver on the ground that performance of the contract is impossible. This says no more than that something unforeseen by either party has intervened to destroy the bargain. On the other hand, if such an eventuality was explicitly covered by the contract, the court would have no trouble requiring the oil company either to deliver from other sources or to pay damages.[8]

---

8. Contracts to buy and sell natural gas at the height of the energy crisis in the mid-1970s are good examples of the problem of foreseeability. Gas-distributing companies were scrambling to secure stable, long-term supplies. As a result, distributors entered into long-term contracts with price escalation clauses. These contracts appeared fair at the time, even from the consumer's point of view. When the shortage of gas appeared to be at crisis level, however, Congress passed the Natural Gas Policy Act, which partially deregulated natural gas prices and made other changes favorable to producers of new gas. By 1982 America was swimming in natural gas because of new exploration, yet the distributors were stuck with long-term contracts that had become extremely unfavorable to consumers. In some places courts are beginning to hold these contracts invalid because circumstances have changed entirely from what all the parties who made the contracts expected at the time. The explicit reasoning of the courts is more complicated than that, but that is the bottom line.

In view of these basic principles of contract law, it is reasonable to conclude that courts will be selective in the marriage contracts they choose to enforce. A marriage contract drafted entirely from the man's point of view, providing that in the event of divorce the woman will receive no property titled in his name and no alimony payments regardless of when the divorce occurs, the number of children involved, or the grounds for divorce, probably would not be enforced.

The court would reason that the disparity of bargaining power was too great and the agreement too one-sided. Yet less one-sided agreements could be entered into as a result of intelligent and evenhanded bargaining, which courts might enforce. For example, a court might enforce the following agreement: the woman gets the children; the man pays a certain sum in child support extended through college and graduate school; the woman receives one-third of all family property but no alimony; and the children are to be educated at certain schools after a certain age. Part of the court's conclusion in this regard might be instructed by the fact that the contract's provisions are not very different from what a court itself would order. Obviously, a court cannot require that children be educated at particular schools or that a father finance his children's graduate school education. It is not unreasonable, however, for a man to agree to pay all educational expenses in return for his wife's willingness to send the children to Saint Paul's.

Furthermore, a marriage contract that regulates property division and alimony only if divorce occurs within a few years of marriage is more likely to be upheld than one that attempts to regulate those questions indefinitely. The birth of children, sickness of either spouse or the children, or changes in the economy would destroy the assumptions on which the initial agreement was predicated. In the business world, with the exception of long-term, secured financing, one seldom sees a contract that extends beyond ten years. The longer the time between the original marriage with its accompanying contract and the actual divorce, the higher the likelihood that a court will decline to enforce the contract.[9]

The purpose of marriage contracts, and even of agreements between people cohabiting on a long-term basis, is to protect at least one party from the courts. Courts probably have more discretionary power in domestic cases than in any other area of law: a runaway court can take almost all the property a man has worked a lifetime to accumulate and give it to his spouse; alternatively, the same court can leave a woman who has contributed her thirty most productive years to family life almost destitute. Placing all one's most crucial personal and financial affairs in the hands of an erratic political hack of a state court judge is terrifying. Judges, after all, are just like doctors: some of them are extremely good, and others will almost certainly kill you.

Nevertheless, courts generally do not like people to protect themselves from courts. Ostensibly the judiciary is in the business of rendering justice. When a party works hard to protect himself from a court, judges worry that he has in

---

9. Reluctance on the part of the courts to give literal effect to old agreements in the face of changed circumstances is common in commercial and property law. For example, we see the application of time principles in litigation concerning oil, coal, and gas leases entered into in the early years of this century before deep-drilling and strip-mining technology were perfected. Although ostensibly the leases in question leased all the oil, coal, or gas on particular property, courts have almost uniformly held that if either deep-drilling or strip-mining techniques are to be employed, the leases must be renegotiated, because the original lessors could not have contemplated these methods of extraction.

mind getting a free hand to do some injustice. Courts have developed numerous devices to protect their own power. The strongest of these devices with respect to contracts is simply to declare a certain type of contract or certain clauses within a contract contrary to public policy. A time-honored but less obvious method of protecting court power is to find unpalatable contracts "vague" and then rewrite them. Other techniques fall in the category of procedural legerdemain—finding that a party waited too long to bring an action on the contract or that a particular defense was "waived" by subsequent conduct are examples. No one can predict which rule will be trotted out in any particular court—or even whether a court will use any protective technique. All that can be said is that even mutually bargained-for marriage contracts or "living-together" contracts are not nearly as trustworthy as are commercial or real property contracts.

Recognition that marriage and "living-together" contracts are difficult to enforce does not mean that they are useless, however. Because almost all domestic hassles are resolved by a settlement and not by in-court litigation, the more ammunition with which a person arms himself or herself for the settlement process, the better the likelihood of a favorable outcome. If a person wants to cohabit on a long-term basis but wants to avoid a Lee Marvin-type palimony suit, it is a good idea to write a favorable formal agreement giving careful attention (and this must be done by a skilled lawyer) to the law of the state where the couple plans to live. If the contract is well drafted, there is better than a fifty-fifty chance that it will be enforceable for at least five years—the period during which things would be about as the people entering into the contract expected.

The same thing goes for a marriage contract between

people getting married for the first time. If, for example, a young woman marries a college senior who has been accepted to medical school, she may be reluctant to quit college herself to work to put him through school. There is nothing unreasonable in this woman's demanding a marriage contract that provides that he will pay her $250,000 if he divorces her in the first ten years and a greater sum if he divorces her later when she is older. Because there is a commercial overlay to this contract—she agrees to support him for seven or more years—it is not unlikely that a court would enforce such a contract.

The marriage contract least likely to be enforced would be one between a forty-year-old, six-figure-income businessman and his eighteen-year-old secretary under which she agrees that if they get divorced she will be entitled to nothing but child support. That does not mean that he should not try to exact such an agreement, however, because it may help him in settlement negotiations. (I am speaking as a lawyer, not as a minister.)

Tнıs chapter has not answered any specific questions about marriage contracts, living together, or palimony. It merely sketches part of the legal perimeter within which the separate state court systems will decide these new issues. Yet the reader should not feel cheated: the most important thing that law schools teach first-year students is that firm answers in the law are dangerous. It is the questions that are important, because they help us to calculate our chances of survival.

Law changes every day in response both to legislative enactments and judicial decisions. Unless a person is a specialist who follows the law's ebb and flow in a limited field on a day-to-day basis, thinking one knows the answers to legal questions can be very dangerous. What a person really needs to know are the appropriate questions so that proper inquiry can be made concerning the law at the exact moment when a given question becomes relevant.

A state court today may hand down a decision enforcing a particular marriage contract while also speaking favorably about them generally in an abstract sort of way. The case generating such an opinion may concern an entirely fair and reasonable contract, but reliance on the opinion's gratuitous discourse (known as "dicta") about the desirability of marriage contracts in general may lead to the drafting of unreasonable, one-sided agreements. Five years from now, when the same court is presented with a different type of contract with different consequences for the parties, the result may be the opposite, and the expectations of persons who relied on the first opinion will be confounded. It is important to know not only what the law is today but also what considerations will affect courts when they decide different cases in the future.

Notwithstanding the tentative nature of my observations, a few concluding comments are in order. First, long-term arrangements where unmarried people live together will eventually spawn a new body of law to protect cohabiting persons in many of the ways that married persons are now protected. Second, the protection afforded cohabiting persons will be substantially less than the protection afforded married persons, and this will particularly be the case if either party is already married. Third, a person who wishes to protect his or her property and income from a potentially devastating divorce judgment is still better off living with a partner of the opposite sex than getting married. Although palimony and property division for housemates present a complicating wrinkle to what was previously a will-and-pleasure relationship, neither of these remedies is likely to be successfully invoked until parties have lived together long enough so that one can fairly say that their relationship became a de facto marriage.

Finally, marriage contracts continue to be alive, well, and extremely valuable in second marriages where they were originally developed to protect the inheritance rights of children. Although they are less reliable in almost all other circumstances, they are still valuable for their use in settlement negotiations and, if fairly drawn, even as enforceable contracts.

It is not my place to make moral judgments concerning the value of marriage vis-à-vis alternative lifestyles. However, I can offer one or two objective legal judgments. Whatever the value of trial periods of living together, once either or both cohabiting partners conclude that they want to spend the rest of their lives together and have children, marriage beats the hell out of its trendy competitors. Marriage cements legally recognizable relationships. For example, if a minor child's legitimate father dies, there is little hassle getting survivors' benefits from the Social Security Administration. If, however, the child is illegitimate, there is no end to the administrative nuisance of hearings and paperwork necessary to get dependent status recognized. This is more true today than in earlier times because Social Security is now looking for ways to reduce its expenses by denying all but ironclad cases for either disability or survivors' benefits.

When two young people have little property, inheritance seems academic, but if the person who owns the family car dies, a cohabiting partner has no rights at all—at least short of hundreds of dollars' worth of legal rigmarole. If an illegitimate child is hurt in an accident, it is problematical whether a putative father can give consent to emergency medical treatment. Furthermore, employer health-care benefits are usually extended automatically to legitimate children but not to the children of one's live-in mate. Most government employee pensions and many private employee pensions automatically provide a reduced retirement benefit for a surviving spouse, but this does not apply to surviving roommates.

The value to older persons of marriage is more questionable from a legal point of view, however. Depending on the level of income, its sources, and the way it is spent, the federal tax law often penalizes marriage. Certainly the Social Security Administration penalizes marriage, so that two elderly retired persons living in a small apartment in Florida may be better off in terms of government benefits if they continue to "live in sin."

Because court-ordered alimony automatically ceases when a woman remarries, a woman entitled to healthy alimony payments should make sure that she negotiates with her former husband for a *contractual* substitute for alimony if she wants to marry someone who cannot support her as well as her alimony awards do. If a husband is paying $2,000 a month alimony to his former wife, he will probably be more than willing to agree to pay her, say, $1,000 a month if she remarries. He saves money and she regularizes her relationship. But if he is obstinate, then "living in sin" again has its rewards, at least in this world.

7

The Bottom Line

PEOPLE have always been tempted to speculate about alternatives to marriage, and in a sense the seeds of today's repudiation of marriage as a sacred rather than a convenient institution have been around as long as marriage has. Yet it is unlikely that intellectual forces alone, without accompanying radical changes in our underlying economic structure, would have caused the wholesale revolution in domestic affairs that we have experienced in the last thirty years. Two economic changes have been most important in producing our new view of marriage: the increased mobility of the American labor force and the expansion of employment opportunities for women.

A successful modern economy requires workers to move in response to the birth and death of industries. For example, in 1945, 17.5 percent of Americans worked on farms; by 1981 only 2.6 percent of Americans were still farmers. Free trade and its attendant domestic and international competition cause both a high mortality rate and a high birthrate for industries. In 1970 only 9 percent of American trade was in the international sector; today we import approximately 21 percent of our products and export approximately 18 percent.

Jobs die in the older, capital-intensive industries like

174

automobiles and steel; jobs are born in the new knowledge-intensive industries like universities, computer software development, telecommunications, and high-technology engineering. If workers do not adapt to these changes, they suffer as individuals and the economy as a whole stagnates.

Both our social and legal structures are designed, therefore, to enhance necessary labor mobility. Strange as it may seem, even some of the United States Supreme Court's controversial criminal law decisions have been crafted to make it easier for poor people to move from one place to another. Before the Supreme Court began to protect people from the police, poor people who drove into new towns in junker cars without any means of support did so at their peril. They were moved on by the cops through a combination of the vagrancy laws and plain harassment. Today vagrancy laws are unconstitutional, and police who harass the poor can be sued in federal court. The Civil Rights Act of 1964 helps overcome impediments to mobility like racial discrimination in hiring, while publicly funded legal aid lawyers bring suits to keep official harassment within tolerable limits.

We have even created a national welfare system that does not penalize recipients when they move from one state to another. People supported by public assistance are encouraged to go where their prospects are brighter, even if that amounts only to trading in Mississippi's parsimonious dole for New York's more generous one. We have affirmative action hiring quotas and prohibitions against making residency for more than thirty days a condition for voting, practicing a profession or regulated calling, or—except in a few narrow cases—working for local governments. No other society has gone so far.

Yet, despite all our efforts to remove barriers to labor

force mobility, the transition for any individual worker from one industry to another is difficult and painful. When high-wage workers lose their good jobs in old industries, they must usually spend many years, often miles away from their original homes, working their way up to another high-wage position.[1] Such forced displacements can be hard on a marriage. On the most obvious level, a two-career household in which one spouse is transferred faces an unenviable choice. Does the one whose job remains follow the partner to the new location and endanger his or her own career? Does the transferred individual give up on that employment and try to find something local? Or do they both try the compromise that would have been unimaginable to our grandparents, the long-distance weekend marriage?

Mobility places other severe stresses on family life. The extended family of yesteryear where three generations lived in the same town and provided one another with reciprocal emotional and financial support is now the exception. Mobility demands that the nuclear family, consisting only of husband, wife, and their unemancipated children, be the modern family unit. For a large segment of our population holidays are the only opportunities for the nuclear family to associate with grandparents and collateral relatives.

This pattern of separation has led us to establish alternative systems to the family for taking care of aging parents, retarded or incompetent children, and others of our kindred who just cannot make it. Social Security, publicly funded residential care facilities, and welfare are all social

---

1. New generations can make the transition more smoothly; few sixteen-year-olds are preparing for a factory job in the steel or auto industries. It is more likely that an ambitious sixteen-year-old who ten years ago would have aspired to a unionized factory job is learning how to operate a computer in a bank or service Japanese and Korean cars.

insurance programs that not only spread more equitably every family's risks in life but that also enhance the mobility of other members of the family. There is little doubt about whether these expenses are necessary; the real question is whether they are sufficient.

The change from the extended family to the nuclear family has both reduced the degree to which the family provides the primary safety net for its members and increased the emotional importance of husbands and wives to each other. Two generations ago husbands and wives typically had their own parents, siblings, and collateral kin to provide emotional support. People were extensively involved with their spouse's extended family, so there were numerous opportunities for positive relationships at different levels. Today, however, we are typically uprooted from this supportive environment, so that when either partner to a marriage fails to provide a total support system for the other partner there is no one else to take up the slack. This means that there will be more divorces and that each instance is likely to be devastating. The rising divorce rate is disturbing evidence that all too many Americans are leading lives of what Henry David Thoreau termed "quiet desperation."

The other crucial economic factor that has encouraged divorce is the opening up of the market economy to women.[2] As I pointed out in Chapter 1, this development is a result of three phenomena: (1) the movement away from capital-intensive production where most jobs entail heavy

2. In the United States women have always done substantial market-sector work. Family farms notoriously use all available family labor, and when America provided extensive agricultural employment women contributed significantly to the production of cash crops. This work differed, however, from the type of market-sector work that women do today; family farm work strengthened rather than weakened the family relationship.

and dangerous work to a diversified economy with numerous service and knowledge-intensive sectors; (2) the development of laborsaving products and machinery that make it possible for today's homemaker to work in the home only fractionally as much as our grandmothers did; and (3) the changing conception of a woman's proper role in society that feminism has spawned.

There was never a shortage of intellectual theories to rationalize free-spirited impulses, but these fundamental changes in the underlying economic structure have allowed us the luxury of experimenting with alternatives to Victorian morality. Freud instructed us about repression, particularly sexual repression; the famous *Playboy* philosophy instructed my generation that women are best treated as recreational objects; and one aspect of the women's movement was that women should be as free as men to engage in sexual experimentation. These intellectual fashions have driven into disrepute the notions of natural order that held sway when economic conditions demanded them and under which sex was related to marriage and marriage was seen as the preeminent device for providing social security. The family still prevails as the focal point of everyone's life in poorer societies like China because there is no alternative; here, however, the existence of alternatives has caused us to lose our former consensus about how men and women should relate to one another, their children, and their community.

We have been experimenting with alternative lifestyles for twenty years, and the society that we have created falls far short of what Freud, *Playboy,* or the women's movement promised us. Nonetheless, the important thing is that we now have had sufficient experience both with the new

economic realities and with the intellectual fashions that changed economic conditions inevitably produced to allow us to reach some tentative conclusion about where we should be going from here.

IT **IS** probably valuable to recapitulate some of the salient facts I presented earlier. The most important of them is the continuing disparity in the earnings of men and women. Feminists argue that any disparity between the earning capacities of men and women is entirely the result of past and present discrimination against women, and much of the disparity can indeed be explained that way. Nonetheless, the fact that occupational segregation of women in low-wage, nonunionized jobs has been resistant to change and that it has actually worsened in the last twenty years—notwithstanding both legal rules forbidding discrimination and social pressure for sexual equality—should at least be taken to mean that enhancing the earning capacity of women is a more difficult task than we thought. Achieving equality in earnings will take far longer than we anticipated a decade ago.

Unfortunately, there are also causes of the earnings disparity that are unrelated to discrimination. Women's lower level of physical strength—with all that implies concerning increased danger from crime—and factors touching on women's responsibilities as primary caretakers of dependent children, which statistics and psychological studies show is usually voluntary, limit their earning abilities. Although we know that discrimination and lack of seniority play a major part in income disparity, it is difficult to determine the relative impact of these socially contrived causes versus other natural or self-induced causes.

The statistics bear repeating because they paint a clear, if bleak picture. The mean wage for women who work full time is 59 percent of the equivalent mean wage for men,[3] and in married households where both husband and wife work full time, the woman's wage on average amounts to only 34.7 percent of the family's earnings. Possibly the most convincing evidence that women's poor performance in the labor force is, in part at least, linked to their parental responsibilities is that previously married women without children average 35.6 weeks of work a year while previously married women with children average only 28.3 weeks of work a year.

As long as we continue to have children, the family will remain the most efficient way of assuring them a decent start in life. The fact that only 1.3 percent of all families with minor children headed by a husband and a wife receive public assistance while 34.3 percent of all previously married female heads of households receive public assistance is dramatic testimony to the economies of scale present in joint households when it comes to child rearing.[4] Further-

3. A recent West Virginia survey indicates that women working full time in my state make only 52 percent of what is earned by their male counterparts. I infer that part of the difference between the national average and the lower West Virginia average comes from the fact that most of our high-wage employment opportunities are still in heavy industry such as coal mining or chemical and glass manufacture. The reverse phenomenon of women earning more than the national average would probably be observed in areas where there are numerous jobs in such fields as administration, publishing, television, and government.

4. There is no reason to believe that the previously married female heads of household who are on welfare come from any different social, educational, or economic background than the married couples who are not on welfare. Never-married female heads of household are measured separately, and among that group over 64 percent receive welfare. It is in this latter group that unwed teenage mothers are counted along with women whose desperate straits may lead them deliberately to have children in order to collect welfare.

more, child care in and of itself often makes single mothers poor; limited job opportunities are not nearly as prominent a cause as the time demands of child rearing standing alone. Only 14 percent of all welfare payments go to families where all children are over twelve, which means that women perform much better economically when they are no longer burdened with dependent children.

The family headed by a married couple is still the basic building block of our civilization. Although serial marriages may be better than no marriage at all from the standpoint of mental health, and produce some economies of scale, they do not achieve the same social benefits as do long-term marriages. When serial marriage is the norm, men must support former wives and their children by them. Both men and women end up taking care of two families if the men actually pay support, but the statistics show that few men actually meet their support obligations in full. The strains on children and other relatives, such as grandparents, are also a prominent reason for preferring one marriage to serial marriages.

Studies of children overwhelmingly support the proposition that delinquency, poor academic performance, and emotional disability all occur more frequently and severely among children from broken homes. One recent government-supported study by Walter Grove of Vanderbilt University and Robert Crutchfield of the University of Washington concludes: "The evidence that the family plays a critical role in juvenile delinquency is one of the strongest and most frequently replicated findings among studies of deviance. However, with few exceptions this evidence has been downplayed by sociologists. The motivation for the de-emphasis of the relationship between the family and delinquency is not entirely clear. [But] . . . this de-emphasis appears to be in part because sociologists have in recent years tended not to see the family as a particularly viable and effective institution and to see divorce as a normal course of action for the modern family."[5] It is as if public authorities downplayed the dangers of drunken driving because people like dry martinis.

In Chapter 4, I related the story of Susan who was trying to support her two children with a factory job. Susan was an unusually strong and well-adjusted parent, but whenever I saw her she was exhausted from the combined effects of night-shift work and daytime child care. Both Susan and her children were uncommonly lucky, however. Susan lived in a small town in West Virginia and had available to her the support network of a real community. Her relatives, friends, and the school authorities provided her with physical and emotional help. In small towns children are exposed to fewer vicious influences than they are in big cities, and when a child begins to wander down dangerous paths that fact is never a secret from his or her parents, neighbors, or teachers. However, the world is not made up of strong parents like Susan who live in small towns.

In my experience, a high percentage of single parents are neither particularly strong nor particularly well adjusted; they often find that they cannot support the dual burdens of being the only breadwinner and the sole parent. When their physical and emotional stamina are finally exhausted, they give up, leaving their children to the mercies of the street. Some streets are meaner than others, and it

---

5. W. Grove and R. Crutchfield, "The Family and Juvenile Delinquency," *The Sociological Quarterly* 23 (Summer 1982), 301–319.

follows almost as surely as night follows day that the lower the economic circumstances of the family, the more malign the street on which the children will be turned out. It is a short step from any such rootlessless to failure in school, truancy, delinquency, and drugs.

It also follows that many children of single parents will find their way to the tavern, the sweatshop, or the itinerant labor force because they lack the family stability, encouragement, and financial help that would cultivate their abilities. We are very good at measuring lost income in households; it is harder to measure lost potential.

Of course, not all children from broken homes fail. Susan's children didn't have problems with delinquency, drugs, or school failure. The point is that divorce *frequently* has an adverse effect on children. Furthermore, when lack of family stability causes failure in school, delinquency, or drug dependency, it is not the family involved who must foot the bill to redeem their troubled children. All the rest of society—through such government social service programs as drug treatment centers, special schools, residential halfway houses, social workers, and probation officers —ends up paying.

When, as is so often the case, the benign social service agencies fail, the courts and the penal system take over. It costs between $14,000 and $25,000 a year, depending on the location, level of security, and the age of the facility, to house a convicted criminal in a prison. The cost of punishment is in addition to the cost to victims of criminal acts. Even if a child is not a delinquent but is simply unprepared for life, we all support him or her through the welfare system.

All this militates strongly in favor of a thoughtful reevaluation of the desirability of divorce. Do we want to continue the morally neutral stand on family matters that has become fashionable in the last ten years? Our current low regard for the family as a necessary institution follows from our adoption of an amiable morality that idealizes a life of passive consumption. Such a view of life necessarily implies the development of social institutions that permit us to shift the responsibility to someone else for children, the elderly, the poor, and the failures and crimes of individuals. The old consensus about the value of long-term marriage had to be destroyed because the new morality demands of its adherents an uncritical endorsement of everyone else's acts.

The viability of the new morality also demands that we reject, ignore, or minimize the existence of certain obvious facts. Preeminent among these facts is that the loss inherent in the dissolution of a marriage is borne by others. Those who work with family law in the courts or social service agencies understand this aspect of the problem, but the majority of people filing for divorce perceive it only dimly, if at all. Were it merely a question of tax dollars the problem would be less severe, but the truth is that the greatest costs cannot be measured in money. Grandparents lose the society of their grandchildren; siblings often lose one another's companionship; fathers become alienated from their children and children lose the guidance and support of their fathers; women become old before their time trying to be both breadwinners and single parents; children feel unloved because they are left unattended; families cease to be natural support systems for their members; and everyone becomes poorer.

In a sense, divorce is like smoking. For years we had a

policy of benign neglect toward smoking despite widespread reports of its harmfulness. Our laissez-faire morality dictated the amiable attitude that it was, after all, the smoker's life. Finally, however, we came to understand that the smoker not only jeopardizes his or her own health but also raises group health insurance rates because a substantial percentage of chronic illness in America is smoking-related. We also came to understand that smokers increase Medicare and Medicaid costs; smokers use scarce hospital beds and personnel resources when they are treated for smoking-related diseases; and smokers often die comparatively young, leaving dependents for the rest of us to support. Consequently, our new approach to smoking is to weigh the individual's right to make a private decision against that decision's harm to society. The result is that we discourage smoking without forbidding it. We have become less amiable and less afraid to make necessary moral judgments.

When it comes to divorce, I do not suggest that we require lawyers to post signs saying "*Warning:* Divorce is Hazardous to Your Health"; nor do I suggest that we resort to coercive measures to discourage divorce. I am suggesting instead that we have made a mistake by not paying greater attention to how our new divorce-on-demand system is affecting a generation of children brought up in the poverty of single-parent homes or, for that matter, how it will affect today's forty-year-old divorced adults when, twenty-five years from now, they need someone to care about them, if not to care for them.

For our purposes divorce cases can be divided into three broad categories. About 20 percent of the time divorce is far and away the best option. Whether the problem is a violent husband, a termagant wife, a chronic alcoholic, or a completely irresponsible spouse, we have all seen marriages where at least one innocent partner and perhaps children will be well served by divorce.

In another 20 percent of the cases divorce will make everyone concerned worse off. These are the marriages where nothing is wrong that a little maturity and mutual accommodation cannot correct; divorce becomes the preferred course of action only because one or both partners have been led to believe that in a marriage anything short of perfection must be resolved by divorce. Sometimes couples who are thoughtlessly headed for the divorce court are saved from folly by friends, ministers, and even lawyers; occasionally a brief period of separation and some hard thinking does the trick. But many couples still needlessly end up divorced because some of our institutions actively encourage divorce as a solution of first rather than last resort.

Sixty percent of divorces fall between the two extremes. When the emotional relationship between husband and wife is considered alone, there is usually justification for divorce. But when the poverty of separate living and the effects on children and grandparents are taken into account, the balance shifts toward staying married. Once these couples make a conscious decision to stay married, the marriage usually improves because a responsible commitment on the part of both partners carries in its wake a resolve to make the best of an imperfect situation.

Few of us who are involved with divorce professionally have any compelling urge to return to the old consensus that enforced Victorian morality before marriage and that punished divorce after marriage. If nothing else, the improvement in birth control techniques allows a relaxation of morality before marriage, which in turn can have the salutary effect of allowing couples to evaluate their compatibility. Promiscuity, with the health hazards it implies, and sex among immature children are practices that should receive greater condemnation than they currently receive, but responsible young adults are probably better off for the opportunities that "trial marriages" allow them. In a similar vein, although divorce is a disaster when it shatters families, staying married under horrible conditions in some cases can be worse than a divorce for all concerned.

We should probably begin to approach divorce the same way we now approach smoking. People can smoke, but we have made sure that they can no longer lie to themselves about the dangers of smoking. Furthermore, by regulating smoking in public places and encouraging people to speak up if smoking annoys them, we have made the social costs of smoking more obvious. The result is that the percentage of young people who begin to smoke has gone down, and many smokers have kicked the habit.

MUCH of the misinformation about divorce concerns its economic implications. Few divorcing couples with children are entirely aware of how poor the dissolution of their joint household will make them. The women are poor because they do not have independent financial means, and this problem is exacerbated by the fact that they must meet the basic needs of their children. The men are poor because according to some divorce court's order they are expected to pay a substantial part of their after-tax income to their former wives. Although the causes of indigency differ, the effect on the quality of life for both spouses is very much the same.

Few people accept poverty graciously. Men don't pay their alimony and child support regularly. Only about two-thirds of the women entitled to support receive anything, and most of them do not get it all. Of course, some men just don't have any money, so there is nothing for a former wife to get no matter how competent the enforcement mechanism is. However, the number of men who cannot pay is small in comparison to the number of men who will not pay. As I explained in Chapter 5, our national system —which is really a decentralized nonsystem—for collecting support is incompetent.

It is possible to create a competent and entirely self-financing system for collecting child support *if* there is the political will. Unfortunately, such political will as exists is firmly in the opposite direction. Congress and the state legislatures are dominated by men. The current incompetent system works with frictionless precision to the advantage of men, their second wives, and even their current sweethearts. No one is as resentful of a man's obligation to support his first wife and her children as his second (or third) wife.

A look at recent sessions of Congress highlights the problem. Bills dealing with a federal system for enforcing child support have been introduced, discussed, debated, reported out of committees, and voted on by one or the other house—but none has been enacted into law. For example, in the fall of 1983 the House of Representatives passed H.R. 4325, entitled "Child Support Enforcement Act of 1983." Essentially, this proposed amendment to the Social Security Act would extend federal enforcement programs that are currently in place for the children of mothers who benefit from the Aid to Families with Dependent Children (AFDC) program to all children regardless of whether they are the beneficiaries of federally funded welfare. When the first session of the Ninety-eighth Congress had adjourned for the year, this legislation was pending before the Senate Finance Committee. In other words, it was still not the law.

During the same session the Senate was considering S. 888, a bill dealing generally with inequities affecting women. Title V of that act also included child support provisions. The legislation would increase the dependent care tax credit to 50 percent for those at the lower end of the economic scale, make the credit refundable for those whose earned credit exceeded their income tax liability, and ease the requirements for child care institutions seeking tax-exempt status. Although the hearings on this bill before the Committee on Finance filled three weighty volumes, once again this proposal remains just that. It is not law.

Several observations are germane on these recent bills. First, although these bills would ameliorate some of the pressures facing single mothers, they are by no means comprehensive. As a practical matter, it is artificial to treat alimony and child support awards as wholly different entities. As I explained, a myriad considerations unrelated to the actual allocation of expenses between spousal support and child support influence the ways in which divorce settlements are drafted. Money may be denominated "alimony" rather than "child support" for tax reasons. Although it is helpful to give single mothers federal assistance in obtaining child support awards, it makes no sense to deny them similar assistance in obtaining alimony. The alimony award may be necessary for the support of their children, and their own material needs can be quite urgent.

The reason the bills never pass is obvious: Congress and the state legislatures are largely inertia machines. Legislative bodies are designed primarily to prevent the passage of bad laws, that is, laws that would enhance the position of one constituency or interest group at the expense of everyone else. Legislatures are organized with the object of defeating selfish predatory legislation sponsored by the well-organized and well-financed jackals of the political jungle. These jackals include union busters; businesses that want to strip-mine in Yellowstone National Park; junk mailers who want the post office to deliver a trailerload of catalogues for the cost of a first-class letter; and people who do business with the government, such as defense contractors. Because ours is a society where most people are, on balance, pleased with the status quo, legislatures are not designed for the purpose of passing good laws. Although our current do-nothing design may have significant long-term advantages over available alternatives, the design itself bodes ominously when there is a need for legislation like a new system of support enforcement.

A legislature cannot be designed without a bias either toward passing too many bad laws or toward passing too few good laws. We have chosen to err on the side of the status quo and pass too few good laws. Any American legislative body, then, is consciously, deliberately, and purposefully designed to pass only legislation that has the broadest possible support. In this regard, it is rare for individual bills on controversial subjects to pass. What actually happens is that packages of bills that accord benefits to different groups pass as part of a grandiose political compromise.[6]

The committee system in Congress and the state legislatures, along with the requirement that bills pass both houses in exactly the same form, make it easy for legislation to come close to passage but never quite make it. For opponents of social legislation, a miss is as good as a mile. For political reasons many legislators must give lip service to bills that they secretly oppose. The attractive feature of all legislatures to their elected members is that the cumbersome mechanics of the process itself guarantees that almost all bills will fail automatically, so everyone can be for everything in confidence that without extraordinary efforts nothing will pass. It does not require a Ph.D. in government to understand that a system like this goes a long way toward providing legislators with job security. Opponents of a bill become an outraged force to be reckoned with only when a bill actually passes. Those who favor a bill, on the other hand, must accept a legislator's representation that he or she supports the bill and will vote for it if it reaches the floor. The shadow play of detailed consideration of bills dealing with support accompanied by occasional passage of such a bill by one house usually suffices to keep legislators on the good side of women's groups.

The secret of legislative inertia is that most bills never reach the floor, and those that do reach the floor of one house reach it in a form different from the form in which they reach the floor of the other house. When each house

6. I have written a book that deals at length with the subject of legislative inertia. The reader who is either suspicious or outraged by my analysis here can find the supporting data necessary to be more persuasive in *How Courts Govern America* (New Haven: Yale University Press, 1981).

passes a different version of a bill, there are endless opportunities for secret opponents to kill the legislation through
the mechanics and delays of the conference committee,
where time often runs out on the legislative session before
the committee bangs out appropriate compromises and reports them to the floor of both houses. In the case of H.R.
4325, for example, the session ended before the Senate
committee reported out any bill. If the Senate approves
some version of H.R. 4325 in 1984, the process will not be
over because the two proposals must then be reconciled.
Yet, since everyone can vote on the floor for *some version*
of the bill, they can all go home and get the votes of the
bill's proponents—who are still hopeful for the next session
—without the bill's ever having passed.

Controversial bills that pass must have the support of at
least a substantial minority; that minority then offers its
support to other minorities interested in other bills. Constituencies that can directly influence elections are generally
able to elicit dedicated and passionate support from legislators. Because constituencies concerned with economic
matters are better financed and better organized politically
than are constituencies concerned with social issues, in any
given Congress or state legislature the lion's share of time
and attention is devoted to economic issues.

Social issues have broad, badly organized, loosely
defined constituencies, whereas economic issues have
narrow, militant, and well-organized constituencies.
Constituencies for social issues have little ability to collect
money from those affected by these issues to finance a good
lobbying effort; constituencies concerned with economic
issues, on the other hand, have enough at stake to support
paid, professional lobbyists who can shepherd bills through

the Byzantine committee process; inform proponents of impending obstacles; explain backroom legislative maneuvering to the constituency's members; and do all the tedious, time-consuming, and expensive staff work that makes legislation happen.

Although the bills concerning enforcement of support have an economic impact, the question of better support for women and children itself falls into the broad "social-issue" category because the affected constituency is not tightly organized or dues paying. In fact, many of the most enthusiastic and best-informed proponents of the legislation are men who have nothing to gain personally from its passage. More important, however, the affected constituency is either unable or unwilling to contribute what little money it has to mount a professional lobbying effort of the type that traditionally gets bills passed. The resources of women's groups for lobbying in Washington are stretched thin, and among many groups issues relating to domestic matters are assigned a lower priority than matters relating to women's opportunities in the market economy.

A further confusing element of the legislative process is that a legislator's public objection to a particular bill may not reflect his or her real objections. When bills are controversial, it is more acceptable to oppose their passage because they "cost too much" than to oppose them because they do something undesirable per se. One of the great sticking points concerning a national system of support enforcement is its cost to taxpayers. The projected fiscal 1984 federal budget deficit is approximately $200 billion, and there is little inclination to raise taxes. For the remainder of the 1980s, therefore, it appears unlikely that Congress will be inclined to create new social programs of any kind, and although a $100 million program is insignificant in comparison to the total federal budget, almost everyone's pet project costs only a few million dollars. As has often been remarked, $100 million here and $100 million there soon adds up to real money.

More efficient enforcement of support obligations would have three distinct effects. First, good enforcement would actually collect cash and pay it over to women and children entitled to it. Second, good enforcement would make it less necessary for enforcement mechanisms to be used at all, since efficiency of enforcement itself encourages voluntary compliance. (Notice how few people drive over fifty-five miles an hour because of the rigor of our current speed limit enforcement.) Finally, and perhaps most important from the long-term perspective, a good system of enforcement would bring the economic disadvantages of divorce home to those who might otherwise approach divorce without regard to its effect on their disposable income. Improved enforcement would make the economic consequences of divorce less dire for working mothers, but it would hardly make divorce a financial windfall. In this last regard, enforcement performs the same function as the surgeon general's warning on tobacco products: it helps to instruct people's understanding of the full dimensions of what they are undertaking to do.

The real objections to more rigorous enforcement are, of course, a logical extension of its advantages. If it becomes easier for women to receive the money to which they are entitled, the balance of power in marriages shifts to some extent. It can be argued that although men may become more reluctant to divorce because they will be hounded efficiently until they pay, women will be encouraged to divorce because the economic penalty they suffer will be less severe. This reasoning sounds logical, but it probably does not comport with real life: the causes of divorce are so complex that more favorable economic treatment of women will probably have a negligible effect on women's decisions to get divorced. As the research data presented in Chapter 3 indicated, women are more concerned with emotional factors like the care of their children than with economic factors. Furthermore, courts are becoming more reluctant to award permanent alimony to women who can work and support themselves. Although alimony and child support may be high while children are minors, unless a woman remarries her financial situation after the children's emancipation will be far less favorable than if she had stayed married. Nonetheless, a good nationwide system of support enforcement would probably require some reevaluation by state courts of the circumstances under which women are entitled to alimony as well as the amounts to be awarded: certainly courts now award alimony in the expectation that only part of it will be paid.

A superb system of support enforcement could be financed from a fund amounting to 5 percent of all awards that are collected. However, everyone affected would need to be a member of the plan. Success would depend on an actuarially sound scheme like group health insurance; if membership were voluntary, the program would be attractive only to high-risk cases and the plan would not be self-supporting. Under such a plan, if a mother is entitled to $500 a month, the fee for collection would be $25; the mother would actually receive $475. Advocates for women are appalled that this charge would be borne by a constituency that is already impoverished, and their outrage is understandable. However, my tactical instincts and experience as a legislator tell me that the cost to taxpayers of the program is currently being used successfully as a reason for doing nothing by people who want to do nothing for other reasons. Few women are paid so promptly and with so little hassle that they would consider contributing 5 percent for an insurance policy a serious imposition.

As in most areas of politics, the principle of the half loaf should be the rule in working for a national support enforcement program. The most difficult part in enacting any piece of controversial legislation is getting Congress to pass the basic skeleton of the program. Tactically, the best technique is usually to settle for enactment of the bare bones— thus getting the principle established and putting the legislation on the books—and then to come back to Congress in subsequent sessions to amend the original legislation.

Although a nationwide system of support enforcement is preferable to a quiltwork of incompatible state enforcement, the fact that hurdles stand in the way of enacting a national system should lead us also to consider opportunities for improvement within states. The problem of paying for such a system at the state level, however, is an even greater obstacle than it is at the federal level, since states —unlike the federal government—cannot print money. Consequently, at the state level cost is a real and not just a chimerical objection. But the same 5 percent charge that I suggest on a nationwide basis will carry the day for any state system as well.

Another change in the current system that would mitigate some of the problems children experience in divorce would be nationwide adoption of West Virginia's primary caretaker parent rule. There is little to be added here to the discussion of the rule in Chapter 3, but it is important to understand that the standards governing child custody are exclusively a state concern, not a subject about which Congress has been delegated the power to legislate.[7] In some states, where the mechanics of divorce litigation are left to the courts under vague statutes, the courts themselves can adopt the primary caretaker parent rule. In other states, such a rule will need to be enacted by statute because there are already specific, detailed statutes covering child custody issues.

The real progress toward which better enforcement and more rational child placement point is a change in attitude. We are a young society with a brief historical experience: in the final analysis, the experiences of the last twenty years will instruct our understanding of what the appropriate cultural norm concerning marriage and divorce should be for a long time to come. The long-term approach that we ultimately adopt is unlikely to be a return to Victorianism, but it will be something other than an amiable, uncensorious laissez-faire tolerance of widespread domestic destruction.

Our current divorce rate is probably attributable in part to our high expectations: we expect jobs with a future; we expect a constantly rising standard of living; and we expect family relationships where the individual benefits always exceed the individual costs. We have not experienced

7. The power to determine proper alimony and child support is also reserved to the state. I advocate federal intervention at the *enforcement* stage because enforcement frequently becomes an interstate problem over which Congress does have jurisdiction.

plagues, foreign invasions, internal revolutions, or oppressive government. Possibly for these reasons we do not have a collective understanding of the inherent sorrow and disappointment of life; we are not conditioned to a refined awareness that some things in life are neither perfectible nor disposable.

Yet even a great cultural advance that gives us a healthy maturity about both marriage and divorce will not give us utopia. Because people are neither perfect nor tolerant, divorce will always be with us. Because law, including family law, is the product of human effort, the solutions it offers will always be flawed. How particular individuals should cope with imperfection is not a subject fit for sublime generalization. The person for whom the be-all and end-all of life is emotional fulfillment will arrive at a different conclusion about his or her marriage than the person who is primarily concerned with personal stability, the next generation, and economic security. If throughout this book I have stressed the disadvantages of divorce, it is not because I reject divorce as a legitimate option for many couples. Rather, it is because dwelling on the disadvantages of divorce raises more of the right questions for a person evaluating that option than does dwelling on its advantages.

I have attempted to examine the forest of considerations that bear on a decision to divorce. The conclusions at which we arrive after an aerial view of the forest are different from our conclusions after viewing individual trees. Forests, however, are an aggregate of trees, and in order to change the forest we must start by changing the trees. Maturity comes to a society after it has come to individuals. Before we turn to massive reforms aimed at restructuring how others live and make moral judgments, we must look inward and responsibly attempt to sort out our own lives.

Index

Abandonment, law of, 44–53
Abstraction, legal (*see* Law, domestic)
Adultery, 47–48, 130–131, 154, 155, 159, 160, 161
Agency for International Development, 136
Aid to Families with Dependent Children (AFDC) program, 188–189
Aldyth, 151n2
Alimony, 1, 4, 5, 7, 9, 10, 12–13, 14, 17–18, 19, 20, 26–27, 30, 32, 36, 45–46, 53, 63, 64, 69, 71, 83, 100, 120–121, 125, 126–127, 136, 139, 140, 142, 143, 161, 162, 164, 167, 173, 187–188, 189, 195, 196n
and deceased husband's estate, 122
enforcement of payment, 109–114, 128, 136–137, 187–188, 189, 195
increase of, 120–122, 127
and lump-sum settlement, 56
and no-fault divorce, 14–15, 49
and periodic payments, 121–122, 127

and taxes, 121–122
(*See also* Palimony)
Altman and Weil (consulting firm), 92
"Amicable" settlements, 119–120
Appellate courts, and domestic cases, 9–10, 33–34, 49, 51, 126–127, 132, 155
Araji, Sharon, 60–61
Arlette of Falaise, 151n2
Atlantic Monthly, x
Attitude, change of, 197–198
Attorneys (*see* Lawyers)

Bachman, Elaine, 61
Blame, blame theory (*see* Fault)
Block, H & R, 94
Bryson, Jeff and Rebecca, 61
Bureau of Labor Statistics, on lawyers' salaries, 90n
Business ownership interests, 138–140, 155–156

Caprice, protection from, 39–40, 41
Chambers, David, 117n

Child-care and women, 60–62,
64–65, 69, 71–72, 80
Child custody (*see* Custody)
Child-snatching, by noncustodial
parents, 114, 117, 118
Child support, 1, 4, 9, 14, 17, 19,
20, 27, 36, 49, 63, 64, 69, 71–
73, 83, 87–90, 100, 101, 104,
115, 118, 121, 126, 136, 160,
162, 164, 167, 170, 195
and enforcement, 1–2, 18, 27,
87–90, 108–114, 115–118,
128, 136, 137, 187–197
multistate compact, 89
lump-sum payment, 52–53
and periodic payments, 121–
122
and remarriage, 107
and taxes, 121–122
Child Support Enforcement Act
of 1983 (H.R. 4325), 188–189
Children and broken homes, 181–
182, 183, 196
(*See also* Custody)
Civil Rights Act of 1964, 175
Cohabitation (*see* Living together)
Common-law marriages, 151, 152,
157
(*See also* Living together)
Community-property states, 36,
53–54, 145–146
Compromise, incentives to, 51
Conciliation and mediation, 135–
136, 143
Condonation, 130–131
Consensus, on marriage and divorce, 1–28, 42, 197–198
and advantages of marriage, 2–
3, 19–20

(*See also* Marriage, economic
and cultural advantages)
and domestic courts (*see* Domestic courts)
fairness and justice, 4–6, 8–9,
10, 17
(*See also* Domestic courts)
and family rights and obligations, 37, 183–184
new developments, 197–198
and old system, 5–9, 10–12,
19, 27, 130–131, 150–151,
184, 186–187
sanctity of marriage, 5, 6, 174
and working women, 7, 10–11,
12, 14, 18, 25–27
(*See also* Domestic courts;
Law, domestic; Living to-
gether; Marriage)
Contract actions, 127–129
Contract law, contractual
clauses, 164–170
Contracts, divorce settlement
(*see* Settlement)
Contracts, marriage, 144–146,
152–154, 161–178
and changing laws, 171–173
and courts, 164–170
and inheritance, 162–164, 172
limited application, 162
one-sided, 164–170
second marriages, 162–164, 172
terms of, 161–170
(*See also* Living together)
Cost of divorce, 54–55, 56, 77,
97–118, 140, 143
and appeal, 107
and child-snatching, 114
and child support, 87–90, 108–
114

Cost of divorce (*cont.*):
  and court costs, 93, 105, 107,
    129–130
  and courts, working of, 100–
    118
  and hiring experts, 107
  and justice, 114–118
  and lawyers' fees, 90–98, 107,
    109, 114–115, 119, 130, 143
  and modifying terms of decree,
    100
  and negotiated settlement, 98–
    100, 104–105
  reforms needed, 115–118
  and remarriage, 105–107
Court orders and divorce, 52, 65–
    66, 96–97, 98–99, 104–105,
    109, 113, 117, 121, 122, 123,
    129, 136, 137, 156–157
  and enforcement, 140
Courts, domestic (*see* Domestic)
Crane, Hart, vii
Credit cards, 42–43
Crutchfield, Robert, 181–182
Custody of children, 1, 2, 4, 7, 9,
    14, 15–20, 23–27, 32, 36, 46,
    48–49, 50, 52–53, 56, 58–86,
    100, 104–105, 115, 120, 137,
    162, 164
  change of, 106–108
  and child-snatching, 114, 117,
    118
  and child support, 72–73
  custody battles and "brain-
    washing," 78–79
  enforcing decisions, 116
  and exhaustive hearings, 81
  explosive issue, 58
  and "fitness," 58–60, 62, 65,
    67–82

  and expert testing, 74–77
  and personal bias, 75
  and primary caretaker parent,
    79–83, 196–197
  joint custody, 69n, 71, 83–86
  maternal presumption, 59–62,
    63–64, 72, 73–74
  measuring and neutrality, 66–
    67
  and remarriage, 105–108
  and settlement out of court,
    62–66, 67–78, 79
  sex-neutral approach and
    women, 64–67, 79–83
  and sexual discrimination, 59,
    80
  and Solomon's wisdom, 38, 64
  speed and permanency of ar-
    rangements, 66
  and strain on children, 66, 76,
    77–79, 81, 83, 86
  temporary, 103
  and working women, 25–27,
    64–65, 72

*Department of Welfare v. Kee-
    see,* 22n
Desperation, quiet, 177
Dibona, Pamela, 61
Disinheritance, 145, 159
Division of labor, 3, 7–8, 60–62,
    147
"Division of Labor Among Co-
    habiting and Married Cou-
    ples, The" (Stafford, Bach-
    man, & Dibona), 61
Divorce:
  decrees, enforcing, 117
  desirability of, 183–187, 188

Divorce (*cont.*):
a disaster, 85, 118, 177, 185, 187
law, previous, 6–9
(*See also* Consensus: old system)
statistics, 1, 37–38, 39, 177, 185–187, 194–195, 197
and poverty, 187–197
Do-it-yourself divorce, 119–120, 123, 129, 141–142
Domestic courts, performance of, 1–2, 3–4, 9–10
adversary process, formal, 31, 32
basic issue in, 41
and children, 15–19, 23–28
contract actions, 127–129, 169
discretion and caprice, 28, 31, 33–34, 39–40, 41, 46, 48–49, 51, 168
economic and emotional aspects, 4–5, 19–20, 25, 56–57, 65, 142, 194–195
and enforcement of support laws, 1–2, 18, 27, 87–90, 108–114, 115–118, 128, 136, 137, 187–197
example of working, 100–118
and "expert" testimony, 23, 74–77, 81, 82, 107
and fault, 4–5, 12–15, 18–23, 25, 26–27, 30, 32, 36
and generational profiles, 9
and "justice," 19–20, 27–28, 33
law and equity, 124–126, 127, 157
and litigant satisfaction, 31, 32, 33–34, 39–40, 117–118

and marriage contracts, 164–170
and measurements, 66–67
and mistreated wife, 18
and old system, 5–9, 10–12, 19, 27, 43–44, 157
and "palimony," 153
powers:
breadth of, 100
limited, 4
and prevalence of divorce, 166
procedural technicalities, understanding, 120–121
rules, procedural and substantive, 130–132
settlement vs. litigation, 52–53, 55–57, 62–66, 67–79, 119–123, 129–133, 134, 135–140, 143, 170, 172
settlement, determining fairness of, 123–129
and sexual morality, 16–17, 82, 151, 154–155
and state statutes, 9–10
suits, problems of, 129–133
translation and retranslation, 29–31, 52
and working women, 12, 14, 15, 18
(*See also* Cost; Custody; Law, domestic)
Domestic law, and lawyers, 91–98, 123–129
Dower, 145

Economic changes and marriage, 174–179
Economic vs. emotional aspects (*see* Emotional)

Economic vs. social issues, 192–193
"Economics of Divorce, The" (Wietzman), 117n
Economies of scale, 148, 181
Edith Swan-neck, 151n2
Education of children, 162, 167
Emotional and economic aspects, 4–5, 19–20, 25, 56–57, 65, 142, 194–195
Emotional support, 3, 4, 20, 45–46, 56–57, 65, 79
(*See also* Custody; Family life)
Equity, 124–126, 127, 128, 157
Estate planning, 163n
Evidence, rules of, 131–132
Expenses, legal (*see* Cost)
"Experts" and court testimony, 23, 74–77, 81, 82, 107
Extramarital sex, 5
(*See also* Adultery)

Family life, supporting network, 3–4, 176–177, 184–185, 186
Family-relations studies, 66, 181–182
Fathers, Husbands and Lovers (Katz and Inker), 60n
Fault, fault divorce, 4–5, 12–15, 18–23, 25, 26–27, 30, 32, 36, 71–72, 130–131, 161
instructive case, 44–53
interesting case, 22n
Fielding, Henry, 151
Flexibility and law, 40–44
Fornication, 154
(*See also* Sex, extramarital and premarital)
Freud, Anna, 66
Freud, Sigmund, 173

Generational profiles, 9
Goldstein, Joseph, 66
Gresham's law of experts, 74
Grove, Walter, 181–182

"Hand-fast" unions, 151n2
Harold Godwinson the Saxon, 151n2
Heckman, Norma, 61
Heisenberg, Werner; Heisenberg uncertainty principle, 67, 70, 71, 86
How Courts Govern America (Neely), 190n
H.R. 4325, 188–189, 191–192
"Husbands' and Wives' Attitude-Behavior Congruence on Family Roles" (Araji), 60–61
Hyatt Legal Clinic, 94–95

Inheritance rights, 148, 157–159, 161, 162–164, 172–173
Inker, Monroe, 60n
Insurance, insurance policies, 30, 55, 122, 123, 150–151, 195
Internal Revenue Service (IRS), 139
(*See also* Taxes)

Joint custody (*see* Custody)
Judges:
incompetent, 39–40, 168
and interpretation of rules, 133
and procedural regularity, 132–133
unpredictable, 71
Jury trials, 124–125, 128
Juvenile delinquency, 181–183

Katz, Sanford, 60n

Labor, division of, 3, 7–8, 60–
62, 147
Labor force, mobility of, 174–
177
Law, domestic, 29–57, 91–98,
123–129
and adversary system, 31, 32
and child custody, 59n
(*See also* Custody)
and complexity of cases, 32–
37, 40, 43
and court translation, 29–31
fair general rules, 38–40
flexibility, 40–44
lawsuits, complications of,
129–133
and lawyers, 91–98, 123–129
predictability, 38–40
principles and specifics, 43–44,
49–50
and property, 53–55
"rule-selection" process, 44–
53
settlement vs. litigation, 52–53,
55–57, 62–66, 67–79, 119–
129, 129–133, 134, 135–
140, 143, 170, 172
and specialization of lawyers,
133–134
technical complexity, 123–
129
three elements, 130
unique element, 34
Law and equity, 124–126, 127
and attorneys' fees, 128
Law, profession of specialists,
133–134

Laws, passage of, 189–194
Lawsuits, problems of, 129–133
Lawyerless divorce, 119–120,
123, 129, 141–142
Lawyers:
competent for divorce cases,
133–137, 140–143
domestic cases, 91–98, 123–
129
fees and income, 90–98, 107,
109, 114–115, 119, 128,
130, 134–135, 143, 153n
hiring; when to hire, 119–123,
130, 133, 136–137, 140–143
legal service, 91, 93–95
public hostility toward, 90–91
and specialization, 133–134
types of, 134–135
Legal clinics, 93–95
Legislative inertia, 189–194
Leofric of Northumbria, 151n2
Litigators, professional, 135
Living together, 146–161
and adultery, 154, 155, 159–
160, 161
and advantages of marriage,
146–150, 158, 161, 172
and business partnerships, 155–
156, 159, 160
and child support, 160
classes of cases, 155–161
and inheritance, 157–159, 161
and legal problems, 151–155
and old morality, 150–151,
154–155, 157, 160
and palimony, 153–154, 156–
157, 159, 169, 170, 172
(*See also* Contracts, marriage)
Lump-sum settlements, 52–53,
56, 137, 139–140

McCall v. Frampton, 155
Making Fathers Pay (Chambers), 117n
Marital roles, proper, 6, 7–8
  (*See also* Consensus; Division of labor)
Marriage contracts (*see* Contracts, marriage)
Marriage, economic and cultural advantages, 2–3, 56–57, 147–148, 158, 161, 172, 181–182
  old system, 5–9, 10–12, 184
  (*See also* Family life)
Marriage, rejection of, 146–148
  (*See also* Living together)
Marriage, role of (*see* Consensus)
Marriage as a sacrament, 5, 174
Marriage, traditional, and economic changes, 174–179
Marvin, Lee and Michelle, 153–154, 169
Maternal presumption in custody decisions, 59–62, 63–64, 72, 73–74
Maturity, individual and social, 198
Mediation and conciliation, 135–136, 143
Mobility of labor force, 174–177
Morality, sexual, 16–17, 82, 154–155
  (*See also* Sex, extramarital and premarital)
Morality, victorian, 151, 178, 186–187, 197

Natural Gas Policy Act, 166
Negotiated divorce (*see* Settlement)

New morality, 183–185, 197–198
  (*See also* Consensus)
No-fault divorce, 13–15, 21, 43, 44, 45, 46, 47, 48–49, 51–53, 68–69, 119

Palimony, 153–154, 156–157, 169, 170, 172
Pensions, pension rights, 30, 55, 138, 139, 143, 148, 149–151, 153, 162, 173
Playboy magazine, 178
Poverty and divorce, 187–197
Premarital sex, 5
  (*See also* Fornication)
Primary caretaker parent, 79–83
"Problems of Professional Couples" (Heckman, Bryson & Bryson), 61
Promiscuity, sexual, 186–187
Property division and distribution, 1, 4, 9, 10, 14, 19, 30, 32, 36, 46, 53–55, 100, 101, 104, 120, 136, 137, 142, 143, 145–146, 150–151, 157–158, 161–162, 164, 167, 171–173
Property rights, real, 148
Prosecuting attorneys, 110–111

Quiet desperation, 177

Rehak v. Mathis, 154–155
Remarriage, and custody, 105–108
Retirement benefits, 149
  (*See also* Pensions)
Robert of Normandy, 151n2

Roman Catholicism, and marriage, 5
Rules, legal, 130–132

S. 888, 189
Senate Finance Committee, 189, 191–192
Settlement vs. litigation, 55–57, 62–66, 67–79, 119–123, 129–133, 134, 135–140, 143, 170
fairness of settlement, court's determination, 123–129
illustrative case, 67–76
and marriage contracts, 172
Sex, extramarital and premarital, 5, 48, 154, 186
(*See also* Adultery)
Sex-neutral systems and women, 64–67
Sexual morality, standards of, 16–17, 82, 151, 154–155
Sexual promiscuity, 186–187
Single parents, single-parent households, 15–16, 74, 85, 147, 182–183, 184
Single-sex couples, 156n–157n
Smoking, new approach to, 184–185, 187, 194
Social vs. economic issues, 192–193
Social insurance programs, 176–177
Social Security, 13, 30, 55, 110, 142, 148, 149, 150, 151n, 153, 161, 162, 172, 176, 188–189
penalization of marriage, 173
Solnit, Albert, 66
Solomon, King, and child custody, 38, 64

Specialization, legal, 133–134
Stafford, Rebecca, 61
Stepparents and custody, 105–107
Storefront lawyers, 94
Student Lawyer magazine, 90n
Supreme Court (*see* United States)

Taxes and deductions, 121–122, 137, 189
corporations, 139
inheritance, 163n
penalization of marriage, 173
Thoreau, Henry David, 177
Title V, S. 888, 189
Trollope, Anthony, 151

U.*C.L.A. Law Review,* 117n
Uniform Reciprocal Enforcement of Support Act, 89, 109–113
United States Supreme Court:
criminal law decisions and labor mobility, 175

Vagrancy laws, 175
Victorian morality, 151, 178, 186–187, 197
Visitation rights, 9, 30, 69, 83, 86, 100, 103, 104, 115, 116, 137, 162

Welfare system, 175, 176–177, 180–181, 183

West Virginia:
  child custody law, 79–86, 196–197
  divorce settlement contracts, 128–129
  marriage laws, 144
Why Courts Don't Work (Neely), 117n
Wietzman, Lenore, 117n
William the Conqueror, 151n2

Women as caretakers, 60–62, 64–65, 69, 71–72, 80
Women, working, 7, 10–11, 12, 14, 18, 25–27, 45, 87, 121, 150, 174, 176, 177–178, 179–181, 182, 184
  and child care, 64–65, 72
  and equality of earnings, 179–180
Women's groups, lobbying, 193

About the Author

JUSTICE RICHARD NEELY is a graduate of Dartmouth College and Yale Law School. He was elected to the West Virginia Supreme Court of Appeals in 1972, where he was Chief Justice in 1980. Between his graduation from Yale and his election to the Supreme Court, Neely served as an Army artillery captain in Vietnam and practiced law in his own one-man office in Fairmont, West Virginia. In 1970 he served one term in the West Virginia Legislature. In addition to his judicial duties, he is professor of economics at the University of Charleston and the author of *How Courts Govern America* and *Why Courts Don't Work.*